MANGIA.... I LOVE YOU

Cook, Eat, Laugh and Love

BY: VICKI MCNICKLE AND LUCY AMICO-PETERS

ISBN-10: 1475129483

ISBN-13: 9781475129489

Contents

Foreword

By Vicki McNickle (Nov 2012)

I haven't always loved the process of cooking. When I was young, learning to cook was born out of necessity more than desire. Mom worked full time most of my childhood (sometimes two jobs!), and the routine was come home from school, clean up the house, make beds and get dinner on. I started with mashed potatoes, then moved to hamburgers, and soon I had advanced to more sophisticated dishes -- pork chops and rice! For a long time, cooking was about "getting it done quickly."

My repertoire expanded greatly over the years as my cooking skills improved, and the joy of cooking started to take hold. By the first edition of this book, I had begun to truly appreciate the joy of cooking for those you love (my son, Taylor, was four at the time), yet I was still running on the get-it-done-quickly model. For anyone who received a copy of the first edition and tried to follow some of the recipes, you most likely noticed that many were missing ingredients or had instructions that were hard to follow. Some just didn't taste quite right. Not testing recipes before you publish a cookbook is a bad idea!

As I reflect back on this, I realize that even though I didn't love the *process* of cooking until later on in life, I always loved the *traditions* around food and cooking with my family and feeding those I care for.

Growing up Italian meant that when family and friends gathered, there was food. It meant that Sunday dinner was at Grandma and Grandpa's house where all my aunts and uncles would gather, cook for hours, and then eat for more hours. It meant baking cookies to give away as gifts at Christmas time and the amazing tradition of Thanksgiving with our whole family.

When my son Taylor was born, I wanted to pass along these traditions to him. I wanted him to grow up with the memories of baking cookies together or waking up to the smell of sauce cooking on Sunday morning. (You will hear a lot about this memory from the family members who have written stories in this book – funny how "gustatory" memories can hold so much emotion!) It was in the years of teaching him that I began to have a greater appreciation for the *art* of cooking. It was in my late 30s that I began to appreciate not only the traditions around food and cooking, but the skill of composing a dish or a meal to please the palate and satisfy the taste buds.

I discovered the artist in myself that loved the creative outlet of cooking. I started to realize there was a lot to learn about cooking, and I was eager to be a student. This is when my real love for cooking started to take shape. It was in my late 40s when I suggested to Mom that we revamp the cookbook, test all the recipes, and do a complete and thorough editing.

After five years of recipe testing, editing, editing, and more editing, the book is finally finished. The week prior to going down to Mom's for Thanksgiving in 2010, I sent her an email saying all the tested recipe edits were in the book, and now we just needed to do final review for clarity and detail in instructions and grammatical editing. We would do that together when I went down the following week to help her with Thanksgiving preparations. (See the Thanksgiving section in the book on our lovely family holiday tradition of celebrating this holiday.)

My husband Tim and I arrived the Saturday before Thanksgiving, and Sunday morning, Mom and I began making canolli shells together – a tradition I had come to love doing with her. When our task was completed, she said she didn't feel well and was going to lie down. That evening, we ended up in the emergency room. When she passed away two weeks later on December 5, my heart was broken. I was not ready for her to leave. I was not done learning from her – getting all my questions answered about her, life, and cooking.

My mother and I shared so many wonderful times together in the kitchen and in life. She taught me so much about how to give with an unselfish heart. How to show love through food and how to be a good person. She showed me what it meant to be a good parent and grandparent -- still waiting to test that second set of skills. Mom loved cooking for her family, and when you arrived at her house, the cupboards and fridge would always have the foods you liked. When my brothers and I all arrived at Thanksgiving, there would always be at least one or two special things for each of us and for the grandkids as well.

Writing this book with Mom was a very special journey that we took together and that has forever changed me. She was not just my mother; she was my friend. We loved to share new things that we learned about life's lessons, the journey of life and ways to maximize its richness. Throughout the process of creating the first edition, and especially as we have worked on this second edition, we shared so many wonderful experiences together.

Throughout the process, I learned much about cooking and discovered wonderful things about our family history. For the first edition, I spent many hours talking with both my mother and my Aunt Sally (Mom's oldest sister) about the recipes in this book, where the recipes came from, and how they themselves had learned how to cook. I learned that my great grandmother in Sicily owned a bakery and found out that my grandfather was quite a culinary expert. These stories are included in many of the recipes.

It is my hope that this book will be more than a place where you can find a recipe; that it will become a thread of connection to and for my family – both immediate and extended family as well as our friends. We share a rich history together. I'd like to think of the stories in this book as the things that keep us together – like the sauce that brings the spaghetti together or the wine that compliments the meal. We share this amazing history that is so much a part of who we are. Even when we don't know those who came before us, they influence and shape us through the traditions we continue to share.

Throughout the book you will find stories written by my Aunt Sally, Uncle Joe and Uncle Angelo, as well as my brothers Harry, Len & Paul on "the love of food". I've also included many family photos that capture some of our rich family history.

May the recipes and stories in this book fill your tummy and your heart. If you were here with me now, I'd cook for you to let you know I care.

The name of the book? My grandmother Marianna Amico, who spoke very little English, used to say when you were done with your first course "Mangia!" Anyone who knew this woman was clear that was she was saying, "I love you." *Vicki*

Dedication and Acknowledgement

This book is dedicated to my mom, Lucy Amico-Peters. I miss you.

Thank you goes to:

My husband Tim for making me a better person and filling my life with joy every day.

My children Taylor, Kari and Kelsey, for never complaining about the weird meal combinations I cooked for them as I was testing recipes. Mostly though, for being really awesome and amazing kids and human beings.

My brothers Harry, Len and Paul – for always having my back – you have no idea how much it means to me.

And finally to my extended family and friends – for your constant encouragement throughout this process.

A special thank you to Len and Astrid Amico, Kelly Machanov, and Denny McGinnis for being recipe "testers" and to Kari McNickle, Kelsey McNickle, and April Miller for being awesome editors! Lastly to Tammy for her photo shop brilliance, Simone for her professional proofreading proficiency, and Patricia Haddock for her editing expertise, and encouraging me to write from my heart.

With love,

Vicki

Notes from Lucy Amico-Peters (Mom)
December 1994

Grandma and Grandpa Amico would be so pleased and proud to know that so many of their recipes are still being used, not only by their children, but also by their grandchildren and some of their great grandchildren. They would be especially pleased to know that one of their grandchildren came up with the wonderful idea of committing those recipes to perpetuity for future generations to enjoy.

Thank you, Vicki, for making this project happen. This cookbook would not have become reality if it hadn't been for your efforts and commitment. You're greatly appreciated and very much loved!

Thanks, also, to all our family and friends who contributed. We appreciate so much your taking the time to submit recipes."

How I learned to cook...

I was 12-years-old when I had my first experience with cooking on my own. Grandma was recuperating from surgery for varicose veins and directed my attempt from her bed. We were going to make spaghetti sauce.

She tried to talk me out of this venture, but I prevailed, and she indulged my wish to prove my culinary skills. Poor woman probably gave in to my pleading only because she was too sick to take a firm stand.

I would take a directive, run to the kitchen, complete that step, run back to the bedroom for directions on the next step and so on. As I think about it, it must have been amusing to her at the time. What I don't recall is if my brothers and father thought the sauce was good!

Most of my learning after that came from observing and asking questions. Sometimes, Grandma would allow me to help. Grandpa was also a pretty good cook and very proprietary about the kitchen. While he liked to help Grandma, he preferred that we didn't get too involved in his creations.

In my teens, I started baking pies. However, not having been able to master the technique of a good pie crust, I would ask my sister Rosie to mix the crust for me. She made it better than anyone!

My mother, too, cooked. My brothers and I loved coming in from school to the wonderful smells of my mother's cooking. Bread baking, sweet potatoes roasting, spaghetti sauce or minestrone or lentil soup simmering away...It was heaven!

Very early on Saturday mornings, Uncle Angelo and I would make our trip to the chicken market and to the butcher shop for the meats that were to be cooked on the weekend. Then, it was the wonderful smells of chicken soup for dinner and liver and onions in wine sauce made with Grandpa's homemade wine for lunch.

Sunday mornings, we would wake to the wonderful odor of onion and garlic being sautéed for the sauce and with the sound of meatballs frying. Grandma always did this before we went to 9:00 AM mass. As you can see, every day and every week were filled with smells and sounds and love of a family who loved to cook for the ones they loved.

Leonard & Marianna Amico
1940's

Appetizers

Kari, Tim, Vicki, Kelsey, Lucy, and Taylor

Florence, Italy

2006

Artichoke Dip

Source: Vicki McNickle

Vicki's note: This recipe is from Bill Suiter - it is always a hit at parties!

- 1 14 oz. can artichoke hearts (water packed), drained and chopped fine
- 2 6 oz. jars marinated artichoke hearts, drained and chopped fine
- 6 tablespoons mayonnaise
- 1 4 oz. can diced mild green chilies
- 1 1/4 cups sharp cheddar cheese, shredded

Preheat oven to 350 degrees.

Mix artichoke with mayonnaise. Spread in bottom of 9" square baking dish. Spread chilies over artichoke/mayonnaise mixture. Top with shredded cheese.

Bake in 350 degree oven for 10-15 minutes or until cheese is melted. Serve with tortilla chips and/or Wheat Thin crackers.

Prep Time: 10 minutes   Start to Finish: 25 minutes   Servings: 6

Artichokes with Lemon & Capers

Source: Vicki McNickle

Vicki's note: On one of our 'fab five' weekends in Santa Cruz we had artichokes similar to this, and after talking with the chef a bit, I was able to somewhat recreate this amazingly wonderful artichoke recipe!

2 large artichokes

1/2 cup kosher salt

1/2 cup sugar

1/4 teaspoon liquid smoke flavoring

2 large lemons, separate use

2 tablespoons olive oil

2 medium shallots, chopped fine

2 cloves garlic, minced

1 tablespoon dried basil

1/2 tablespoon dried parsley

1 tablespoon capers, rinsed and drained

1/2 cup white wine

2 tablespoons butter

Cut the top 1/4 off the choke, and snap off the outer leaves until you reach pale green, soft leaves. Snip off sharp tips that may remain. Cut choke in half and using a spoon, remove the hairy choke from the center and discard. Immediately plunge into large bowl of cold water to which the juice of one lemon has been added (you can throw in the rind of the lemon too). This step avoids discoloration. Repeat with remaining artichokes. Drain the artichokes and spin to dry.

In a large pot, mix 3 quarts water, sugar, salt and liquid smoke. Bring to a boil. Add prepared artichokes, and cook on a low boil for 10-15 minutes, or until knife can easily be inserted into bottom. NOTE - do NOT overcook - you don't want them to be mushy.

Remove from water and let drain on paper towels.

While artichokes are cooking, heat oil over medium low heat in frying pan large enough to accommodate the four artichoke halves. Add shallot and sauté until translucent - about 3-5 minutes. Add garlic and sauté one more minute - do not brown. Add wine, basil, parsley, capers and juice from second lemon. To the pan, add the cooked, dried artichoke open face down. Spoon some of the sauce over the artichokes. Cover pan and simmer for 5 minutes to let the artichokes absorb the flavors. Add butter and let it melt.

Serve artichokes with some of the sauce from the pan.

Servings: 4

4

Caponata

Eggplant appetizer
Source: Lucy Peters

Lucy's note: Eaten with Italian bread, provolone cheese and pepperoni, this is a taste treat that will harden your arteries and bring a smile to your face!

Vicki's note: Mom started making this from scratch for Thanksgiving several years ago. My brothers and I all love it, and so appreciate the care and time mom took in making it. Much better than what you get from a can!

3 tablespoons olive oil, divided
1 medium onion, chopped
2 medium celery stalks, chopped
2 cloves garlic, minced
1 pound eggplant, peeled and cubed into 1/2" pieces
1 large tomato, chopped
3 pimiento-stuffed green olives, halved
2 tablespoons capers, rinsed
2 tablespoons red wine vinegar
1 teaspoon sugar
2 tablespoons pine nuts, toasted
1 teaspoon salt
1/2 teaspoon pepper

Heat 2 tbsp. olive oil in large pot. Sauté onion, until soft and translucent. Remove from pan and set aside. Next add celery to pot and sauté for 8-10 minutes. (Celery should have some firmness to it). Remove from pan and add to bowl with the onions. Add garlic to pan and sauté about 1 minute, adding a little more oil if needed. (NOTE: Don't overcook or brown, otherwise the garlic will be bitter). Remove from pan; add cooked garlic to bowl with onion and celery. Heat 1 more tablespoon oil in pot, then place eggplant into pot and sauté until translucent and somewhat soft - 10 to 15 minutes. Add onion, celery, and garlic back to pot. Stir and simmer for about 5 minutes. Add tomato, olives, capers, vinegar and sugar. Cover and simmer for about 15 minutes.

Uncover and simmer for additional 5 to 10 minutes or until most of liquid has evaporated. Season to taste with salt & pepper. Cool slightly; add pine nuts.

Cover and chill overnight. Serve at room temperature with crusty Italian bread. Caponata will keep in the refrigerator for up to a month, or may be frozen for up to 3 months. Defrost in refrigerator before bringing to room temperature for serving.

Prep Time: 30 minutes   Servings: 10

Cardoon

Fried Burdock
Source: Lucy Peters

Lucy's note: Cardoons are part of the artichoke family, but look like very large celery heads. Raw, they are bitter. Parboiling eliminates the bitterness.

Vicki's note: Thanksgiving would not be complete without cardoon! It is a funny scene in the kitchen. Mom, Paul and I are making the cardoon - a bit of a lengthy process as you will see - and you watch everyone descend on the kitchen like vultures to grab some while they are hot just after they've been taken out of the pan. Often, by the time we get each batch out, the previous one has been eaten! We learned a long time ago to eat some as we are cooking or we'll never get any! But really - - - it always warms your heart when the people you love are eating your food.... it's an Italian thing! I recall this as being one of my brother Paulie's favorite foods!

2 quarts water
1 large lemon
2 pounds cardoons, ends
   and leaves trimmed
4 medium eggs
1 cup flour
1 teaspoon salt
1/2 teaspoon pepper
1 tablespoon parsley
1/8 cup Romano cheese
6 cups vegetable oil,
   used in batches

Put large pot of water to which 1 Tbsp. salt has been added to boil on high.

In a bowl, combine the water, lemon juice and rind (just put squeezed lemon rind in water). Using a vegetable peeler, remove the tough outer strings of the cardoon ribs. Cut the ribs into 2-inch lengths, adding them to the lemon water as you work. Drain the cardoon ribs, transfer them to the large saucepan of boiling water and cook until very tender, about 30 minutes. Drain and pat dry; let cool.

While cardoons are cooking, beat eggs in a large bowl. Whisk in flour, salt, pepper, parsley and cheese. Whisk with fork until fully incorporated - consistency should be like that of thin pancake batter. If too thick add small amounts of water to reach desired consistency. Drain cardoons on paper towels. Let cool, and dry off with paper towels.

Heat about 1 1/2 inches oil to 360 degree in a 4- to 5-quart heavy pot over medium heat. Dip cardoons in batter, lifting out coated cardoon 2 at a time, letting excess drip off, and then carefully drop into hot oil. When all of batch has been added, fry, turning occasionally, until golden, 2 to 4 minutes. Do not overcrowd pan - do a few at a time. Transfer with a slotted spoon to fresh paper towels to drain. Season with salt as they come out. Coat and fry remaining cardoons in 4 batches. (Return oil to 360 degrees between batches.) Serve as an appetizer or snack.

Serving Ideas: If you cannot find cardoon (also known as burdock) you can use artichoke stalks as they have a similar taste and consistency. Grandma Amico made this a little differently - she dipped the cardoons in beaten eggs first, then into the flour mixture and then fried them.

Prep Time: 30 minutes   Start to Finish: 1 hour 30 minutes   Batches

Clam Dip

Source: Lucy Peters

1 cup cottage cheese,
  may be low fat

1/2 cup cream cheese, at
  room temperature

2 6 oz. cans chopped
  clams, drained

1 tablespoon lemon juice

1/2 teaspoon
  Worcestershire sauce

1/4 teaspoon dried dill weed

1/4 teaspoon garlic powder

1/2 teaspoon parsley

Salt and pepper, to taste

Drain cottage cheese in a strainer lined with cheese-cloth if you have it; otherwise just let it sit in strainer a bit longer. Press out as much moisture as possible

Place in blender with cream cheese and blend until smooth.

Place mixture into serving bowl; stir in remaining ingredients. Refrigerate for about one hour. Serve with vegetables and/or crackers.

Prep Time: 15 minutes   Start to Finish: 1 hour 15 minutes   Servings: 8

Clams Casino

Source: Lucy Peters

Vicki's note: Making clams casino when we get together for Thanksgiving has been a tradition with our family for years. My niece Leah has taken to being the master of this project, and does a great job making them!

2 tablespoons butter

4 tablespoons lemon juice

1 1/2 teaspoons parsley flakes

3 slices bacon, cooked crisp and crumbled

2 6 oz. cans chopped clams, drained (reserve 2 Tbsp of the juice)

1 1/2 tablespoons freshly grated Romano cheese, divided use

1/4 cup Italian flavored bread crumbs

1 tablespoon onion, finely diced

1 teaspoon green bell pepper, diced fine

1/4 teaspoon garlic powder

Pre-heat oven to 350 degrees.

Cook bacon, set aside. While bacon is cooking, melt butter in microwave in small bowl. Stir in lemon juice and parsley into melted butter. Set aside. .

In a medium mixing bowl, combine drained clams, bread crumbs, onions, bell pepper, and garlic powder, 3 tablespoons of lemon/butter/parsley mixture and 1 tablespoon of the cheese. Mixture should be moist, but not watery. If more moisture is needed, add some of the reserved clam juice, a little at a time, until desired consistency is reached. Note: if you are like mom, you may not like bell peppers, in which case you can substitute finely diced celery for the bell pepper.

Fill 6 to 8 large clam shells with clam mixture, topping each with a bit of the bacon. Drizzle 1 1/2 tablespoons of remaining lemon/butter/parsley mixture over shells.

NOTE: If you don't have clam shells, aluminum foil that has been folded in half and formed around a 1" ramekin makes a great substitute. Fill with about 2-3 tablespoons of filling.

Bake for 10 minutes. Change oven setting to broil. Drizzle remaining lemon/butter/parsley mixture over each clam and sprinkle with remaining cheese. Place under broiler until cheese is lightly browned. Watch carefully to avoid burning cheese. Serve hot.

Prep Time: 20 minutes   Start to Finish: 30 minutes   Servings: 8

Crab Canapes

Source: Lucy Peters

Vicki's note: These are a delicious treat to serve as party appetizers. Mom got this recipe from a friend she worked with many years ago. It was a big hit with all the Miller clan from the first time we tasted them!

3 ounces cream cheese, at
   room temperature

2 tablespoons mayonnaise

1/4 cup Romano cheese, grated

4 ounces mozzarella
   cheese, shredded

2 green onions, thinly sliced

1 6 oz. can crab meat, lump crab
   in can or frozen works as well

1/2 teaspoon salt

1/4 teaspoon pepper

1/4 teaspoon hot sauce

1 tablespoon fresh lemon juice

6 English muffins, cut in half

Preheat broiler. Mix together cream cheese, mayonnaise and Romano cheese until well combined, then stir in shredded mozzarella cheese, green onions and crab meat. Add salt, pepper, hot sauce and lemon juice. Stir until fully incorporated.

Under broiler, lightly toast the tops and bottoms of English muffins. Once cool enough to handle, spread 1/2 of mixture onto each English muffin half. Broil on second rack below boiler until bubbly, about 5-7 minutes. Keep an eye on them to make sure they don't burn. Serve hot.

Serving Ideas: English muffin halves may be cut into fourths after broiling and served as hors d'oeuvres.

Prep Time: 10 minutes   Start to Finish: 15 minutes   Servings: 6

Fried Zucchini *or Eggplant or Artichoke Hearts*

Source: Lucy Peters

2 cups all purpose flour

1 teaspoon baking soda

1/2 teaspoon salt

1/4 teaspoon pepper

1 teaspoon dried parsley

1 teaspoon dried mint flakes

3/4 cup water

1/2 teaspoon lemon juice

3 tablespoons olive oil

4 large zucchini, sliced 1/2" thick (or 2 eggplant or 1 package frozen artichoke hearts)

2 cups vegetable oil

Mix flour, baking soda, 1/2 teaspoon salt, 1/4 teaspoon pepper, parsley and mint flakes in a large bowl. In a small bowl, whisk together water, 1/2 teaspoon lemon juice and olive oil, add to flour mixture. Whisk to combine ingredients. Consistency should be like thin pancake batter. If batter becomes too thick, add small amount of water to reach proper consistency. Set aside.

Sliced zucchini rounds, eggplant slices and frozen artichoke hearts may be dipped in this batter. To prepare vegetables:

FOR ZUCCHINI: Wash and dry. Cut off ends and slice 1/2 inch thick rounds. If moist, pat dry before proceeding.

FOR EGGPLANT SLICES: Lightly salt and place in a colander to drain for 30 minutes, rinse and pat very dry before frying.

FOR ARTICHOKE HEARTS: Defrost in the refrigerator. Remove from package and dry thoroughly.

Heat the vegetable oil in a large frying pan to 350 degrees. Dip cooled and dried vegetables into batter. Shake off excess. Carefully place into hot oil and fry for 2 to 3 minutes per side until golden brown, Remove to paper towels to drain. Sprinkle with salt as soon as you take them out of the oil and place on towels. Cool slightly and enjoy as either appetizer or side dish. If using as an appetizer, eggplant may be cut into fourths. Serve while still warm.

Prep Time: 15 minutes   Start to Finish: 45 minutes   Servings: 4

Garden Shrimp Dip

Source: Lucy Peters

2 cups plain nonfat
  yogurt, drained
1 envelope vegetable
  soup mix, dried
1 cup cooked shrimp, tiny
1/4 cup chives, chopped

Drain yogurt in colander lined with cheesecloth for about 1/2 hour over a bowl - making sure bottom is not touching the liquid that is draining out.

In a medium bowl, combine drained yogurt, soup mix, shrimp and chives. Cover and refrigerate for at least 2 hours, ideally 4 hours.

Serving Ideas: Serve as a dip with vegetables or crackers.

Prep Time: 35 minutes   Start to Finish: 2 hours 35 minutes   Servings: 8

Guacamole

Source: Paul Miller, Jr.

4 cloves garlic

1 small onion

1/2 jalapeno, seeded
and deveined

1 plum tomato, seeded
and quartered

1/4 cup cilantro, stems
removed juice of 1/2 a lime

1 teaspoon pepper

2 teaspoons salt

1/2 teaspoon ground cumin

5 avocados

In a food processor chop garlic, onion, jalapeno and tomato. Add cilantro, lime juice, spices and 1 avocado. Blend until mixture is slightly chunky but almost smooth.

In a separate bowl, seed remaining avocados and remove from skin. Add mixture from food processor and mash into avocados. Stir until blended, retaining chunky consistency.

Serving Ideas: Serve with chips or on the side with any Mexican meal!

Prep Time: 15 minutes

Hummus

Source: Denny McGinnis

Vicki's notes: This recipe is from my dear friend Denny. She has an uncanny ability to make the simple taste wonderful!

2 16 oz. cans garbanzo beans, drained; reserve liquid

1/4 cup sesame tahini, more if you want more taste

2 cloves garlic, diced

3 tablespoons lemon juice

1 1/2 teaspoons fresh mint, chopped, or 3/4 tsp dried

1/4 cup reserved garbanzo juice

Salt, to taste

Place all ingredients into blender. Add a little of reserved liquid from beans. Mix to smooth consistency, adding more liquid as needed. Let chill. Serve with pita squares or no-fat tortilla chips (this is the low-cal version).

Serving Ideas: You can also spread this in a pita pocket with some cucumber, lettuce and tomato for a great sandwich.

Prep Time: 10 minutes

Servings: 8

Josephinas

Source: Lucy Peters

Lucy's note: This is from my friend and great cook, Kelly (Reid) Machnov, who lives in Walnut Creek, CA. She worked with us at Marshall A. Peters Accountancy Corp., in Marina Del Rey, CA. in the early '80s and used to bring these in for all of us to enjoy. She has remained a loving friend, with whom I still share recipes and with whom I share an addictive interest in politics.

1 4 oz. can green chiles, diced
1/4 pound butter, softened
1 cup Monterey Jack
cheese, shredded
3 French baguettes

Preheat oven to 350 degrees.

Cut baguettes in half lengthwise. Place on cookie sheets lined with parchment or aluminum foil. Place all other ingredients into blender or food processor. Process until smooth. Divide mixture into six parts.

Spread each half of baguette with one part of mixture. Place pan(s) in oven for about 5 minutes or until lightly browned. Serve hot.

Serving Ideas: This recipe is great for entertaining.

Prep Time: 10 minutes   Start to Finish: 25 minutes   Servings: 10

Mushroom Turnovers

Source: Vicki McNickle

Vicki's note: This recipe is originally from Diane Boney...our dear friend from Buffalo. When I think of Diane, I always remember her with a smile on her face and a kind word. Dennis, Mr. Boney, was always forthcoming with a joke in his charming southern style. They now live in North Carolina.

9 ounces cream cheese, softened
1/2 cup unsalted butter, softened
1 1/2 cups flour
1 tablespoon butter
1 medium onion, finely chopped
1/2 pound mushrooms,
  finely chopped
1/4 teaspoon thyme
1/2 teaspoon salt
1/4 teaspoon pepper
1/8 cup sour cream
1 egg white, well beaten

Preheat oven to 425 degrees. Prepare cookie sheets by either spraying with cooking spray or lining with parchment (better choice).

DOUGH: In a large bowl mix together cream cheese, butter and flour thoroughly until smooth. Cover bowl with plastic wrap and chill for 30 minutes or more. While dough is chilling prepare filling.

FILLING: sauté onion in 1 tablespoon butter for 5 minutes. Add mushrooms and continue sautéing for another 2 minutes. Add thyme, salt, pepper and sour cream to pan. Stir well; remove from heat.

Remove dough from refrigerator. On floured surface, roll out dough to 1/8" thick. Cut into 2" rounds with biscuit cutter or juice glass. Spread 1/2 tablespoon filling in center of each round. Fold over to create a crescent shape. Seal by pressing edges with a fork. Poke a small slit in top of each turnover with a sharp knife to vent while cooking. Place turnover on baking sheet, and brush tops with well beaten egg white.

Place turnovers on baking sheets and bake for 15 to 20 minutes. Remove from oven when lightly browned. Cool on wire rack.

Serving Ideas: May be made ahead and frozen until ready to bake. If frozen, allow to thaw slightly, then proceed with above baking instructions.

Prep Time: 1 hour   Start to Finish: 1 hour 20 minutes   Servings: 10

Mushrooms Parmesan

Source: Lucy Peters

1 pound medium
  mushrooms, sliced
5 tablespoons butter,
  separate use
3 tablespoons flour
3/4 cup milk (warmed)
3/4 cup cream, warmed, or
  evaporated milk warmed
1/2 teaspoon salt
1/4 teaspoon pepper
1/4 teaspoon nutmeg
1/4 cup Italian flavored
  breadcrumbs
1/2 cup Romano cheese, grated

Pre-heat broiler.

Melt 2 Tbsp. butter in large frying pan on medium heat. Add mushrooms and sauté until they are almost cooked. Remove from heat.

In a medium pan, melt 3 tablespoons butter on low heat, blend in the flour and stir with wooden spoon for 1 minute to let flour cook. Make sure to not let it burn. Add milk, cream, salt, pepper, and nutmeg and cook stirring until thick.

Place mushrooms in a casserole dish and pour sauce over top. Sprinkle with cheese and breadcrumbs. Brown under broiler for a few minutes. Serve hot.

Olive Cheese Balls

Source: Vicki McNickle

Vicki's note: This recipe is from my Aunt Louise on my Dad's side. I remember the first time Mom made these I thought I'd died and gone to heaven! I have served these at parties many times over the years, and they are usually the first thing to go.

2 cups sharp cheddar cheese, shredded (8 oz.)
1 1/4 cups flour (not self rising)
1/2 cup butter, melted
30 pimiento-stuffed green olives

Preheat oven to 400 degrees.

Combine cheese and flour. Mix in butter; work dough with hands if it seems dry. Mold 1 tablespoon dough around each olive. Let stand in refrigerator for 1 hour.

Bake in 400 degree oven for 15 to 20 minutes. Balls will be just golden.

Serving Ideas: Serve warm as an appetizer for party treat.

Salsa Fresca

Source: Paul Miller

Vicki's note: This is a GREAT salsa recipe from my brother Paul – he knows how to make great Mexican food. Check out his Carne Asada recipe for a real treat.

5 medium plum tomatoes

**1/2 jalapeno pepper,
  seeded and deveined**

1 medium sweet onion

1/3 cup cilantro, stems removed

1 tablespoon olive oil

1/2 teaspoon pepper

1/2 teaspoon salt

1/4 teaspoon ground cumin

1/2 teaspoon garlic powder

1 medium lime, juiced

Halve the tomatoes and squeeze out the seeds. Remove the seeds and ribs from the jalapeno and chop into small chunks. Cut the onion into small chunks. Remove the large stems from cilantro and chop. Add all ingredients to a food processor and combine briefly for a chunky salsa.

NOTE: Paul prefers to hand chop all ingredients and use a hand crank processor that allows him to achieve the perfect, chunky salsa Fresca.

Serving Ideas: Serve with tortilla chips.

This salsa can also be used to make a great ceviche! Cover a 3/4 pound orange roughy fillet with lime juice in a sealable container, and let marinate in the refrigerator overnight (8 to 12 hours minimum). Rinse the fillet lightly and then chop or shred the fillet. Mix with salsa fresca and serve.

Prep Time: 35 minutes

Vegetable Bars

Source: Shirley McNickle

Vicki's note: This recipe is from my mother-in-law Shirley. These veggie bars are a big hit with our kids and are a great appetizer to serve when you have a lot of company. Very easy to make.

2 tubes crescent rolls, 8 count each

3/4 cup mayonnaise

1/2 cup sour cream

2 8 oz. packages cream cheese, softened

1/2 envelope ranch salad dressing

1/4 teaspoon garlic powder

1/4 teaspoon onion powder

1 teaspoon dried dill weed

3/4 cup green bell pepper, chopped into 1/2" pieces

3/4 cup green onion, chopped into 1/2" pieces

3/4 cup carrot, chopped into 1/2" pieces

3/4 cup cauliflower, chopped into 1/2" pieces

6 radishes, sliced thin

3/4 cup cheddar cheese, shredded

Preheat oven to 350 degrees F. While oven is heating, cover bottom of 11" x 17" baking pan with the sheets of crescent roll dough, patting and stretching to fit and making sure there are no holes or gaps in the dough. Bake in oven for 7 to 8 minutes, or until lightly browned. Remove from oven and let cool.

In mixing bowl, combine mayonnaise, sour cream, softened cream cheese, ranch dressing and spices through dill weed. Mix well to combine - the consistency should be smooth. Set aside.

Chop all vegetables as directed and combine in bowl until mixed.

Spread cream cheese mixture on top of cooled pastry in baking pan. Top with mixed vegetables. Top with grated cheese.

Cover pan with plastic wrap and gently push vegetables down into cream cheese mixture. Chill in refrigerator for 3 to 4 hours.

Cut into bars to serve.

Prep Time: 30 minutes   Start to Finish: 3 hours 30 minutes   Servings: 12

Lucy Amico-Peters, Angelo Amico, Joe Amico, Sam Amico, and Sally
Amico-Tudini

1970's

How I learned to cook...

Most of my learning was from my Grandmother Rosaria (my mother's mother), who we called "Nanna Saridda." We lived with her when I was age 13-15, and she did most of the cooking. I used to follow her around the kitchen and ask questions all the time. She was very organized and very precise.

While Nanna Saridda owned a cookie shop when my mother was a little girl, her other cooking was mostly improvised. She liked to try new ways to cook vegetables and meat, and she made the best minestrone soup. When I make minestrone today, I always remember how she used to "clear out" all her leftover vegetables and add them to the soup. She would add a "pinch" of this or that, and a "bit" of this or that, and always olive oil and, of course, garlic.

Nanna Saridda used to roast garlic by wrapping it in brown paper and placing it on the hot plate in the old-fashioned stove that was used for both cooking and heating. She would then spread the softened, roasted garlic on bread and drizzle olive oil over it. Oh, so good! Sometimes she would use the roasted garlic on pasta or vegetables. She mashed the garlic and added salt, pepper and olive oil to it before using it with pasta or vegetables. She also used it when roasting red and green peppers. These were wonderful eaten by themselves, in a sandwich or with just plain bread.

I could go on and on about the wonderful memories I have of learning to cook and eating Italian. I learned by being persistent and with Nanna Saridda being so loving and caring. To this day, I think of her with much love in my heart.

Breads

Harry, Vicki, Len, Lucy and Paul
Phoenix, AZ mid 1990's

Banana Nut Bread

Source: Lucy Peters

Vicki's notes: Mom got this recipe from one of the people she used to work with at the Meyer Hospital (early '70s). This is by far my favorite banana nut bread recipe. I love the moist center and slightly crispy outside!

1 3/4 cups flour, sifted

2/3 cup sugar

1 teaspoon baking soda

1/4 teaspoon salt

2 eggs, well beaten

1/4 cup milk

1/2 cup butter, room temperature

1/2 teaspoon vanilla

3 bananas, mashed

1/2 cup walnuts, chopped

Preheat oven to 350 degrees. Put walnuts on a shallow cookie sheet, and toast for 7 minutes. Remove from oven and cool. Once cooled, chop nuts (not too fine - you want "pieces" not crumbs). While nuts are baking, you can continue putting together your cookies.

Lightly coat loaf pan with cooking spray on bottom and sides. If you don't have cooking spray, use vegetable oil (do not use olive oil).

While nuts are toasting, you can put together your bread. Sift dry ingredients (flour, sugar, baking soda and salt) together in medium bowl. Set aside. In large bowl, gently beat together eggs, milk, butter, vanilla. In batches, add to dry ingredients and mix thoroughly after each addition. Stir in mashed bananas. Stir in nuts. Pour into loaf pan which has been sprayed with cooking spray. Bake in 350 degree oven for 55 minutes or until toothpick inserted in middle comes out clean. Let cool on a wire rack. Remove from pan once cooled by sliding knife along sides of pan.

Prep Time: 15 minutes

Cornbread Supreme

Source: Len & Astrid Amico

Lucy's note: My niece Sarah sent us this recipe. Sarah lives in North Carolina and is my nephew Len Amico's daughter. I understand she enjoys cooking.

2 cups flour

1 cup sugar

1 cup yellow cornmeal

4 teaspoons baking powder

1 cup milk

4 eggs, beaten

1 cup butter, melted and cooled

Preheat oven to 350 degrees. Prepare 9" x 13" baking pan by spraying with cooking spray. Set aside

Measure all dry ingredients into a large mixing bowl. Whisk to blend and then create a well in the center. In a separate small bowl beat together egg and milk. Pour milk and egg mixture into the well and mix until liquid is incorporated, being careful not to over mix. Stir in cooled butter.

Pour batter into prepared pan; bake for 30 to 35 minutes. Toothpick inserted should come out clean.

Serving Ideas: Recipe can be halved and baked in an 8" x 8" square pan.

Prep Time: 30 minutes   Start to Finish: 1 hour   Servings: 8

Pumpkin Nut Bread

Source: Vicki McNickle

Vicki's note: This recipe is from Mom. An old time favorite at Christmastime.

2 cups flour

2 teaspoon baking powder

1/4 teaspoon baking soda

1/2 teaspoon salt

1 teaspoon cinnamon

1/2 teaspoon nutmeg

Pinch cloves

Pinch ginger

1 cup packed brown sugar

1/3 cup shortening

1 cup canned pumpkin

2 eggs

1/4 cup milk

1 cup toasted chopped pecans

Preheat oven to 350 degrees. Grease one standard size loaf pan on bottom and sides with cooking spray.

Mix together flour, baking powder, baking soda, salt and spices in a bowl; set aside.

In a separate bowl, cream together brown sugar and shortening. Add pumpkin and beat on medium-low speed for 30 to 45 seconds until sugar, shortening and pumpkin are fully incorporated. Add eggs one at a time, beating after each until incorporated. Add milk and beat and additional 45 to 60 seconds. Add dry ingredients and mix a little at time until blended. Fold chopped pecans into batter and pour mixture into prepared loaf pan.

Bake in 350 degree oven for 55-60 minutes or until toothpick inserted in the center comes out clean.

Serving Ideas: This bread freezes well. If you are not going to use it all at once, slice, wrap in plastic wrap, and place in an airtight container or sealed plastic bag.

Sausage Bread

Source: Sally Tudini

Vicki's note: This recipe is affectionately known as Great Grandma Rosaria's Sausage Bread - but I figured it was easier to find as Sausage Bread! Aunt Sal tells me that this bread was a holiday tradition when she was a girl. It was a much favored holiday treat for her.

1 tablespoon cornmeal

1 package active dry yeast

1/2 cup warm water

1 cup warm milk

1 teaspoon sugar

2 teaspoons olive oil, divided use

2 1/2 cups all-purpose
flour, divided use

1/2 cup whole wheat flour

1 teaspoon salt

1/2 pound sweet Italian sausage

1/2 medium onion,
finely chopped

1 egg, beaten with 1
teaspoon water

Preheat oven to 375 degrees and sprinkle baking sheet with 1 tablespoon cornmeal.

DOUGH

This dough can be made in a bread machine if you have one. Follow the instructions for your bread machine through the kneading phase. However, our grandmothers didn't have such things, and some of us may not either, so here is the long version, step by step.

In a large bowl, sprinkle yeast over warm water. Let stand until proofed--about 5 minutes. Into yeast and water mixture stir milk, sugar and one teaspoon of oil. Set aside.

In another large bowl, mix 2 1/2 cups all-purpose flour, 1/2 cup wheat flour and salt. Add liquids to flour mixture and combine using a spatula or your hand until smooth and elastic (about 5 minutes). You may need to add an additional 1/4 cup more of all-purpose flour if the dough is tacky or sticky.

Turn dough out onto a lightly floured board. Knead until dough is smooth and satiny and small bubbles form just under the surface (about 15 minutes). Add more flour if dough becomes sticky. [Note: your bread machine should take you through this step.] Turn dough into a lightly greased bowl. Cover and let rise in a warm place protected from drafts until doubled in size (about 1 hour).

COOKING SAUSAGE AND ONIONS

While dough is rising, remove sausage from casing and crumble into large frying pan. Add chopped onion. Brown meat and onion lightly over medium heat, stirring often until sausage is cooked through and onion is translucent. Remove meat and onion and let cool and drain on paper towel.

ASSEMBLY AND COOKING

Once dough has doubled, place on a lightly floured breadboard, and roll the dough into a 10" x 14" rectangle. Spread the cooled sausage mixture over the dough, leaving a 1-inch border around the edges. Brush the 1-inch border of the dough with the egg and water mixture (egg wash). Starting at a long end, roll the dough, jelly roll-style, into a log shape, pinching the edges closed as you roll.

Place the bread, seam side down, on the prepared baking sheet and brush the top of the bread with the remaining egg wash. Brush dough with the remaining teaspoon of oil and let rise for about 30 minutes. Bake in 375 degree oven for about 30 to 35 minutes or until crust is golden brown and loaf sounds hollow when tapped.

Prep Time: 1 hour   Start to Finish: 2 hours 30 minutes

St. Joseph's Day Bread

Source: Lucy Peters

Vicki's note: The celebration of St. Joseph's day as it was done in my mother's family started in the small towns of Italy. Those who wanted to participate in the "devotion" would prepare a feast of meatless dishes. St. Joseph's day is March 19th and is in the middle of lent. Mom would talk about Grandma Amico making this bread when she was little.

1 1/2 cups warm water

2 packages dry yeast,
  NOT rapid rise

2 tablespoons vegetable
  shortening

1 tablespoon sugar, or honey

1 tablespoon butter, softened

2 teaspoons salt

4 1/2 cups all-purpose flour

1 egg, beaten

In large bowl, combine first 6 ingredients (water to salt). Set aside for 5 minutes. In the meantime, in bowl of electric mixer (or other large bowl), place 2 1/2 cups of the flour. Add yeast mixture. Using paddle attachment, stir to incorporate ingredients (low speed). Keeping speed of beaters at low speed, add enough of remaining flour to form dough. Change to dough attachment. Continue to "knead" dough (at medium low speed), adding additional flour as needed, until dough is stiff and smooth.

Remove from bowl; knead by hand a few times. Shape dough into a ball. Place in a lightly greased bowl, turning dough to coat all sides. Cover bowl with a kitchen towel and place in a draft-free location until dough has doubled in size, about 1 hour. Punch dough down; cut into 6 equal pieces. Place on a parchment lined cookie sheet; cover and allow to rest for 10 minutes. Roll each piece of dough into 12 inch long ropes. Braid 3 of the ropes to form a long braid. Do the same with second 3 ropes. Shape the two braids into wreath shapes. Spray cookie sheet with canola oil spray. Place loaves on sheet, cover and let rise in a draft-free location, until doubled in size, about 30 minutes.

In the meantime, preheat oven to 400 degrees. Brush top of loaves with egg. Bake the loaves for 25 to 30 minutes or until golden brown. If you're unsure if bread is baked, tap bottom of loaf. It should sound hollow when done. Remove bread from baking sheet and allow to cool on wire rack.

Prep Time: 2 hours 50 minutes   Start to Finish: 3 hours

Joe Amico, Lucy Amico-Peters, Angelo Amico

Note from Joseph Amico (Uncle Joe)
December 1994

Learning to cook...

I found very early in life that my mother had a pipeline to the gods! Now, how did I know that?

Ever since I can remember, there were special days--a weekday or a Sunday--when an aroma that I can only describe as heavenly would invade my nostrils. And so, with a child's curiosity, I would drag the chair to the stove to seek the whereabouts of this intoxicating aroma. As I stood on tiptoe, lo and behold, there was a sea of bubbling, red liquid! I could have stayed there forever, inhaling to my heart's content. But then Ma's voice would shake me out of my trance, "Joe, chefa!"

I implored her to let me help her the next time she made succo. God love her, she taught me how. She taught me everything-- how to chop the onions, sauté the onions and garlic for the sauce, break the eggs, grate the cheese and soak the bread for the meatballs. The most fun was digging my hands into the mysterious meatball mixture. I still love the texture, the feel, and I was ever so proud that I was Ma's little helper!

The last years were filled with warm and poignant memories. I think I can still smell Ma's succo! Sunday mornings were extra special since the delicious odor of cooking succo permeated the house. This forced us out of bed, rushing to get a slice of Grandma's freshly baked bread, carrying that slice gently to the bubbling pot of succo, dipping it into the delightful liquid, first one side of the slice and then the other, and devouring the whole thing in one bite. Ma would of course admonish us, fearing Pa would catch us. Fortunately, he never did!

Today Ma's sauce still lives on... as it is traditional in my house to cook sauce using Ma's recipe at least once a week.

And so, Ma, wherever you are, you will always be a very special part of all of us! To you Ma, Fara Brindisi a la Pasta con Succo!

Breakfast

Tim's Family – Rick, Emma, Carol, Shirley, Julie, Rachel, Denise, Bradley and

Tim

"The McNickles and Bullocks"

Stafford, KS - Christmas 2007

Vicki's Note: My mother-in-law and sisters-in-law have both contributed

recipes to the cookbook.

Artichoke Frittata

Source: Sally Tudini

1 package frozen artichoke hearts, or canned artichokes, rinsed well and patted dry

3 tablespoons olive oil, more as needed

1 teaspoon butter

1 small onion, or 3 to 4 shallots, finely chopped

1 clove garlic, finely minced

1/2 teaspoon dried mint flakes

1 teaspoon dried parsley

1/2 teaspoon dried basil

8 medium eggs, beaten

1/2 cup milk

1/2 teaspoon Tabasco sauce

1 teaspoon salt

1/8 teaspoon pepper

1/2 cup grated Romano cheese, divided use

2 tablespoons fresh basil, chopped (optional)

Defrost artichoke hearts by placing into colander in sink for 1/2 hour or put in bowl in refrigerator for few hours. Once thawed, thoroughly pat dry with paper towels. Cut into quarters. They should be bite-sized pieces. SEE NOTES for other vegetable ideas if you would like to substitute other vegetables for this recipe.

Heat a large frying pan over medium heat. Add 2 Tbsp olive oil and 1 tsp butter. Once butter is melted, sauté finely chopped onion until translucent. Add minced garlic and herbs (mint, parsley and basil); sauté for 1 minute more. Remove from pan and set aside.

Sauté artichoke in same pan for 2 to 3 minutes. Remove from pan and set aside.

In large bowl, combine eggs, milk, salt and pepper. Stir in 1/4 cup of the Romano cheese. Add onion, garlic, herb mixture, Tabasco sauce and artichokes to eggs. Stir well. Add more oil and butter to pan, if needed. Pour mixture into heated pan. Reduce heat to low. As egg mixture begins to set, lift edges gently to allow eggs to run underneath. Cover pan and continue cooking for 12 minutes. In the meantime, preheat broiler, moving rack to middle position of oven.

Remove cover from pan and place pan under broiler until top is lightly browned. Watch carefully. Sprinkle with remaining Romano cheese and chopped fresh basil (if using). Transfer to large serving platter and cut into wedges.

Serving Ideas: Serve with fresh Italian or French bread and a side of fruit salad.

Other vegetables may be substituted for the artichokes – see suggestions below

CAULIFLOWER: Parboil one cup of bite-sized flowerets. Add cauliflower and 1/2 cup Italian seasoned breadcrumbs to egg mixture. Proceed as above.

SPINACH: Steam 2 tightly packed cups of spinach for 2 minutes. Remove with slotted ladle. Squeeze water out of spinach until almost dry. Chop into bite-sized pieces; add to egg mixture along with optional cooked crumbled bacon (amount is up to the cook). Proceed as above.

POTATOES: Peel, cut into small cubes and boil until barely tender. Drain and dry, then sauté with onion until potatoes are cooked. Proceed as above.

These are just a few of the variations on the Frittata theme. Almost any vegetable may be substituted or added to the Artichoke Frittata.

As an added bonus, all of these are wonderful as cold sandwiches (on a crispy roll or Italian bread).

Prep Time: 15 minutes   Servings: 6

Egg Breakfast Casserole

This recipe is prepared the night before and refrigerated   *Source: Vicki McNickle*

Vicki's note: This dish reminds me of Thanksgiving in Lake Arrowhead. Mom made it on several occasions when we were all together; it went a long way to feeding all those hungry bodies! It brings back memories of warm cozy mornings in a house on the lake.

1 pound Italian sausage

8 eggs, beaten

2 cups milk

1 cup cheddar cheese, shredded

2 slices bread, cubed

1 teaspoon salt

1/4 teaspoon pepper

3/4 teaspoon dry mustard, or 1/2
   teaspoon prepared mustard

Remove sausage from casings; cook over medium heat, breaking it up as it browns. Remove from heat; drain well on plate lined with paper towels. Set aside.

Beat eggs well with milk. Add cheese, bread, salt, pepper and mustard, and sausage - stir gently to mix. Pour into 9" x 13" casserole dish; cover and refrigerate overnight.

In the morning, remove casserole from refrigerator; turn oven to 350 degrees and place casserole in oven BEFORE oven preheats. Adding dish to a cold oven prevents the casserole dish (assuming it is glass) from exploding in the oven. Bake for 40 to 45 minutes. Remove from oven and cover with aluminum foil; allow to set for about 10 minutes before cutting into squares to serve.

Prep Time: 20 minutes   Start to Finish: 1 hour 15 minutes   Servings: 8

Eggs with Potato and Onions

Source: Lucy Peters

3 teaspoons vegetable
   oil, divided

1 large potato, peeled and cubed

1/2 teaspoon salt, divided

1/4 medium onion,
   finely chopped

8 eggs

1/4 cup milk, or half-and-half

1/4 teaspoon pepper

1 teaspoon dried parsley

1/4 teaspoon dried mint flakes

Peel and cut potato into small cubes. Heat a large skillet on med-high heat. Add oil and heat 45 seconds. Add potato - do not stir for 2 minutes! - Then add 1/4 tsp salt and stir. Continue cooking, stirring occasionally until browned and almost cooked through (about 10 minutes). Then add 1 tsp oil and finely chopped onions. Cook until onions are translucent.

While potato and onions are cooking, beat together eggs, milk, 1/4 tsp salt, pepper and herbs.

When potato and onions are cooked, add eggs. Stir, and cook until eggs have reached desired doneness.

Serve with salsa on the side if desired.

Prep Time: 10 minutes   Servings: 4

Fried Eggs & Bologna

Source: Paul Miller, Sr.

Vicki's note: When we were kids, fried eggs and bologna were the ultimate treat! This simple but delicious recipe brings back many fond childhood memories.
When Mom was a girl, Grandma would chop up the bologna and scramble the egg...she says it was the best!

1 teaspoon butter

1 slice bologna

1 egg

2 slices bread

1/2 teaspoon ketchup

Heat butter in a medium sized frying pan. When melted, add bologna. Making a small slit on one side of the slice of bologna will prevent it from curling as it heats up. Cook (turning once) until just beginning to crisp.

Set cooked bologna aside. Cook egg sunny side up or over easy if you prefer. While egg is cooking, toast bread.

Place egg and bologna on top of one slice of bread, add ketchup and top with other slice of bread and chow down!

Prep Time: 10 minutes   Servings: 1

Grandma Lucy's Pancakes

Source: Lucy Peters

Vicki's note: When the grandchildren would go to visit Mom, she would make them 'grandma pancakes' for breakfast.

2 cups Bisquick baking mix

1/4 teaspoon salt

1/2 teaspoon baking powder

1 cup milk

2 large eggs, separated

1 teaspoon pure vanilla extract

1 tablespoon canola oil

1 tablespoon melted butter

1 teaspoon white sugar,
   for egg whites

Whisk together baking mix, salt and baking powder. Set aside.

In a small bowl, whisk together milk, 2 egg yolks, vanilla, oil and butter. Pour into dry ingredients. Stir gently to combine. Set aside. NOTE: With pancakes, you want to leave the lumps in - so don't over mix.

In a non-metal bowl, beat egg whites until soft peaks form. Add 1 teaspoon sugar. Continue beating until stiff peaks form. Gently stir 1/2 of egg whites into batter. Fold remainder of egg whites into batter.

Pour 1/4 cup batter onto a hot, lightly greased griddle or skillet that has been heated on medium. Cook until the pancakes have a bubbly surface and slightly dry edges. Turn and cook other side until golden brown. Serve with warm maple syrup and butter.

Serving Ideas: Other optional toppings include butter and powdered sugar or a fruit compote.

Prep Time: 15 minutes   Start to Finish: 45 minutes   Servings: 5

Spinach Omelet

Source: Lucy Peters

Lucy's note: Grandma Amico often served this as a side dish when we had lentil soup or any of the other meatless pasta dishes. Leftover omelet was often taken to school in a sandwich

1/2 package frozen spinach, cooked and drained completely. Can substitute 1 cup fresh cooked if desired, but drain as well.

8 eggs

1/2 teaspoon salt

1/4 teaspoon pepper

1 tablespoon dried basil, 2 Tbsp if fresh

1/8 cup Romano cheese

1 tablespoon olive oil

1 clove garlic, minced

Cook spinach according to package directions. Let drain in colander in sink until liquid is gone - you will need to press the spinach down in the colander a few times to get out the excess moisture.

Turn on broiler.

Beat eggs with salt, pepper, basil and HALF of the Romano cheese. In an oven proof pan, heat oil over med-low. Sauté minced garlic in olive oil about 1 minute - do not let it brown or burn. Add drained spinach and sauté for 3 to 4 minutes. Add egg mixture. Allow to set on bottom of pan without stirring for about 3 to 5 minutes. With a spatula, gently lift the sides of the egg mixture and tilt pan to allow egg mixture on top to run underneath. Continue to do this until eggs are almost completely cooked. Remove from stove top; sprinkle with additional Romano cheese and place under broiler for about 2 min - until cheese is bubbly and slightly browned. Transfer omelet to large plate and cut into wedges.

Serving Ideas: This omelet can also be made with cauliflower or ricotta. If using cauliflower, prepare as here, but instead of adding spinach, add the cauliflower. If adding ricotta, drain 1/2 cup of excess moisture in colander, and add stir in with egg mixture.

Prep Time: 15 minutes   Start to Finish: 25 minutes   Servings: 4

Angelo Amico & Lucy Amico-Peters – visiting together for the first time the town where their parents Marianne & Leonard Amico married and lived for several years before coming to the United States. This is also the town where Sam, Sally, Rosie & Joe Amico were born... Serradifelco, Italy 2009

Notes from Angelo Amico (Uncle Ange)
December 1994

On the love of food...

Among the fondest and most treasured memories of childhood certainly would have to be the smells of home. It was the magic of the culinary creations at the hands of my mother that I reflect upon to this day, in awesome wonder. It is something I still miss very much.

This woman could take a potatoes, some onions, a few peppers, a pinch of this and a dab of that, chop in some leftovers, and fix it so you swore she just created some new, gourmet dish that would be a total success in a fancy restaurant.

Without question, though, the one, all-time, greatest of all the smells of home and the one to die for (even to this day) is the unmistakable, heartwarming, mouthwatering, most loved smell of homemade bread baking in the oven.

The gloom of a bad day at work or a poor test result at school along with the cold, wintery walk home seemed to somehow instantly disappear the minute you walked through the door of home and were greeted with the wonderful smells of Mama's kitchen.

Sam Scarpelli (right) is a dear friend of Lucy's. To the far left is his partner
Richard Perez, and in the middle is Carol Miller and Lucy Peters
Mid 90's Phoenix, Az.

Bonnie Butter Cake

Source: Virginia Amico

Vicki's note: Aunt Gina used to make this cake for birthdays. It's rich but worth all the calories!

2/3 cup butter, softened

1 1/2 cups sugar

2 eggs

1 1/2 teaspoons vanilla

2 3/4 cups all-purpose flour

2 1/2 teaspoons baking powder

1/2 teaspoon salt

1 1/4 cups milk

Spray and flour two 9" layer pans or one 13" x 9" oblong pan. Set aside. Preheat oven to 350 degrees.

Cream together softened butter and sugar. Add eggs one at a time, beating to incorporate after each. Add vanilla and beat on high speed until fluffy - about 5 minutes, scraping sides of bowl occasionally.

In a separate bowl, sift together flour, baking powder and salt. Mix dry ingredients and milk alternately into creamed butter mixture on low speed until fully incorporated

Pour into prepared pan and bake for 35 to 40 minutes. Cake is done when toothpick inserted in middle comes out clean.

Let cakes cool completely on wire rack. Once fully cooled, cake can be topped with your favorite frosting. Chocolate was always a hit in our house!

Serving Ideas: Egg substitute may be used in place of eggs or use one whole egg and 2 egg whites. Fat free or 1% milk may be substituted for whole milk.

Carrot Cake

Source: Lucy Peters

Vicki's note: This is a great version of carrot cake Mom modified to make her own! At one time she took up cake making and decorating as a hobby - quite lovely stuff got created.

3 cups all-purpose flour, sifted

1 1/2 cups sugar

1 teaspoon salt

1 tablespoon baking soda

2 teaspoons ground cinnamon

1 1/2 teaspoons ground nutmeg

1 1/2 cups corn oil, or canola

4 large eggs, room temperature

1 tablespoon vanilla extract

1 3/4 cups chopped walnuts,
   toasted (separate use)

3/4 cup shredded coconut meat

3 cups shredded carrot

1 cup crushed pineapple,
   drained well

1 cup golden raisins, optional

CREAM CHEESE FROSTING

1 (8 oz) package cream cheese,
   room temperature

6 tablespoons unsalted
   butter, room temperature

1 1/2 teaspoons vanilla extract

3 cups powdered sugar, sifted

Preheat oven to 350 degrees. Grease 2 - 9 inch cake pans. If you have it on hand, line each cake pan with parchment paper (bottom only) - it makes the cake come out easier. Spray parchment paper lightly with cooking spray. Set pans aside.

Sift dry ingredients into bowl. With beater on low, add to flour mixture - oil, then eggs one at a time, beating to incorporate after each. Then add vanilla. Beat well. Fold in 1 1/4 cups of the walnuts (reserve other 1/2 cup for garnish), coconut, carrots, pineapple, and raisins (if using). Pour batter into prepared pans. Place on middle rack of oven and bake for 30 to 35 minutes, or until toothpick inserted in center comes out clean.

Cool cakes in pan on cooling rack for 10 to 15 minutes. Remove cakes from pan and continue to let cool completely on rack for about three hours.

While cake is cooling, prepare cream cheese frosting (see recipe below). Once cake is frosted, sprinkle remaining 1/2 cup walnuts over top of cake.

Cream Cheese Frosting

Beat cream cheese and butter together with electric mixer until well blended. Stir in vanilla. Gradually add powdered sugar a little at a time until fully incorporated.

Frost cake and sprinkle top with remaining chopped walnuts.

Serving Ideas: This recipe may also be baked in 9" x 13" baking pan; increase total baking time to one hour.

Prep Time: 15 minutes   Start to Finish: 1 hour   Servings: 10

Pound Cake

Source: Lucy Peters

Lucy's note: Another of Mae Syracuse's (Aunt Gina's Mom) wonderful baked goods recipes.

2 cups butter, softened

2 cups sugar

9 small eggs, 8 if they are large

2 tablespoons brandy

1 teaspoon vanilla

1/2 teaspoon nutmeg

4 cups cake flour

1/2 teaspoon salt

1/2 teaspoon cream of tartar

Preheat oven to 325 degrees. Grease and flour 2 loaf pans.

In a large bowl, beat butter while slowly adding sugar, beating until sugar is fully incorporated into butter. Add eggs 1 at a time until each one is fully incorporated. Add brandy, vanilla and nutmeg, and continue beating until fully incorporated. Set aside.

In a separate bowl, sift together flour, salt and cream of tartar. Add flour mixture gradually to the liquid ingredients, and beat on low speed just until thoroughly incorporated.

Pour batter into pans. Bake for 60 minutes or until toothpick inserted in center comes out dry. Cool cakes completely before serving.

Serving Ideas: Serve this yummy pound cake with sliced strawberries or peaches that have been lightly sprinkled with sugar. Another great treat is to slice a loaf in thirds, and put cannoli filling in between each layer and then some on top. VERY good!

Prep Time: 15 minutes   Start to Finish: 1 hour 20 minutes   Servings: 16

Texas Sheet Cake

Vicki's note: This recipe was given to Mom when she was working at St. Luke's Hospital in Phoenix, AZ in 1975.

2 cups flour

2 cups sugar

1/2 teaspoon salt

2 sticks butter (16 tablespoons)

1 cup water

4 tablespoons cocoa

2 eggs, beaten

1/2 cup milk

1 teaspoon white wine vinegar

1 teaspoon baking soda

1 teaspoon vanilla

FROSTING

1 stick butter (8 tablespoons)

4 tablespoons cocoa

6 tablespoons milk

1 pound powdered sugar

1 teaspoon vanilla

Pre-heat oven to 375 degrees.

Sift flour, sugar and salt together in large bowl. Set aside.

In medium sauce pan, bring 2 sticks butter, 1 cup water and 4 tbsp. cocoa to boil (over medium heat). In meantime, beat together the 2 eggs, 1/2 cup milk, vinegar, baking soda and 1 tsp. vanilla in a small bowl.

Add melted butter mixture to flour mixture. Stir well. Add egg mixture and stir well. (Mixture will be hot). Pour into greased 11" x 17" jelly roll pan (or cookie sheet) and bake at for 20 minutes let cool for 5 minutes, then pour frosting over top. Let cool in pan and cut into squares to serve.

FROSTING

While cake is baking, make frosting. This is important to do now, as unlike other cakes, this frosting goes on while the cake is hot.

Bring butter, cocoa and milk to boil. When mixture is boiling, add the powdered sugar and stir until smooth. Remove from heat and stir in vanilla. Spread topping on cake while cake is still hot (about 5 minutes after removing from oven).

Prep Time: 45 minutes   Start to Finish: 1 hour 5 minutes

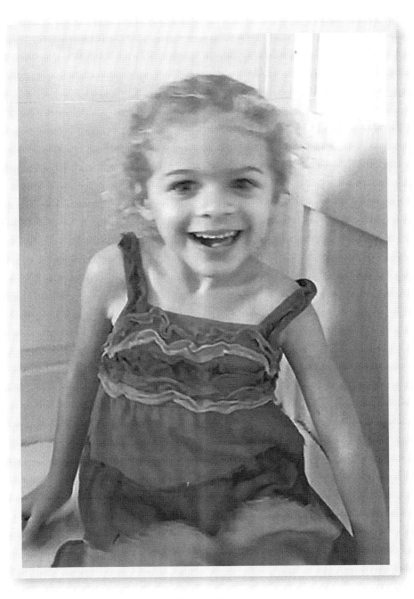

Claudia Miller
Born January 2011
Daughter of Harry Miller and Cynthia Starr

Notes from Harry Miller
January 2012

Lucy's oldest son

Cooking, a passion, a need, a pleasure...

In our family, food has always been a time for coming together – a time when we gathered to share our love, our day and our lives as no other time could afford.

On Sundays, our entire family would gather at Grandma and Grandpa's to enjoy each other's company, the love of our family, and the delicacies of my Grandmother's kitchen. These are some of my earliest memories of cooking–not by me, but by Grandma, Mom and her sisters as they prepared the day's feast. My favorite memory of these times (and there are many I'll always cherish) was waking up at Grandmother's house early Sunday mornings to the smell of onions and garlic cooking as she started her pot of sauce. To this day, Sunday morning is my favorite time to cook a pot of sauce. The other was dunking bread into the pot after it had been cooking for a few hours–nothing like it in the world! It was in Grandmother's and Mother's kitchen that I gained an appreciation for cooking that I feel blessed to have experienced.

Learning to cook came early in our teens with Mom and Dad teaching us to prepare parts of our dinner before they came home from work. This was something we all took turns doing. One of our first jobs was to peal, slice and cook potatoes for dinner. I can't tell you how often we did this, then we would rush off to play and promptly forget about the potatoes—only to find 45 minutes later, the water had boiled off, and the potatoes were scorched on the bottom of the pot. Man, what an ugly odor! Funny stuff in retrospect although Mom wasn't too amused at the time.

Learning to really cook came in small doses, and that was fine. When I moved from home, all the bits and pieces learned over the years began to come together–both out of necessity, and quite honestly, for the fun of it. I can't tell you how many times I called Mom or Vic to get one recipe or another or ask for advice on how to prepare a certain food. Their advice was blessed and wonderful!

What I've found over the years is that I love to cook for all kinds of reasons. To please myself and to try something new or something fondly remembered, or to please those who are our guests, or just for fun. I'm even having a little fun teaching our fourteen-month-old daughter, Claudia, to cook as she sits and eats a rice cracker and I talk to her while preparing food. She giggles and babbles; it's great fun.

In the end, cooking brings a certain comfort to life that's difficult to describe. Maybe it's a combination of all of the above that creates a particular pleasure. I'm happy to admit in my next life, I'm coming back as a rotund chef.

Vicki & Lucy

This is the town where Leonard and Marianna Amico were married and lived
until they moved to the United States. Same place where Joe, Sally, Sam and
Rosie were born.

Serradifalco, Sicily Italy 2004

Banana Drop Cookies

Source: Shirley McNickle

Vicki's note: These cookies that their Grandma Shirley makes are a favorite of Kari and Kelsey.

1 1/4 cups white sugar

2/3 cup shortening

2 eggs, room temperature

1 teaspoon vanilla

1 cup bananas, mashed
  (about 3 whole)

2 1/4 cups flour

2 teaspoons baking powder

1/4 teaspoon baking soda

1/2 teaspoon salt

1 cup raw walnuts

1/4 cup sugar

1/2 teaspoon cinnamon

Preheat oven to 350 degrees. If using nuts, put walnuts on a shallow cookie sheet, and toast for 7 minutes. Remove from oven and cool. Once cooled, chop nuts (not too fine - you want 'pieces' not crumbs). While nuts are baking, you can continue putting together your cookies.

In a large bowl, cream sugar and shortening on low speed of mixer. Add eggs and vanilla and mix until incorporated. Stir in mashed bananas.

In a separate bowl, stir together flour, salt, baking powder and baking soda. Add in batches to sugar and banana mixture, stirring to combine after each addition. Stir in nuts.

Refrigerate for 1 hour or overnight, covered.

In a shallow bowl, mix together 1/4 cup sugar and 1/2 teaspoon cinnamon. Form dough into 1 1/2 inch balls and roll each in cinnamon sugar mixture. Place 1 inch apart on a baking sheet that has been lined with parchment.

Bake at 350 degrees for 12 to 15 minutes until golden brown on bottom.

Prep Time: 15 minutes   Start to Finish: 1 hour 30 minutes

Biscotti

Italian Biscuit Cookies
Source: Vicki McNickle

Vicki's note: This recipe is a combination of several recipes I have tested and this is my unique "spin" on biscotti, which means "twice baked cookies." When I was little Grandma Amico always had biscotti in the bread drawer - given their shape I used to call them "banana cookies."

1/3 cup unsalted butter

1 cup sugar, or 3/4 cup sugar
   and 1/4 cup almond paste
   (see recipe and notes below)

2 eggs

1 teaspoon vanilla extract

1 teaspoon anise extract

1 tablespoon ground anise seeds

2 1/2 cups flour

1 1/2 teaspoons baking powder

1/2 teaspoon baking soda

1/8 teaspoon salt

1/2 cup almonds, toasted
   (whole or chopped)

ALMOND PASTE

1 cup whole almond

1 cup sugar

1/4 cup water

1/3 teaspoon vanilla extract

1/2 teaspoon almond extract

1/8 cup powdered sugar

COOKIES

Preheat oven to 350 degrees. Toast almonds for 6 minutes (both for base recipe and almond paste if you are using) remove from oven and let cool.

If using Almond Paste, make first - recipe below. This can be made and refrigerated for up to two weeks in the fridge. While almonds are cooking, beat together butter and sugar until fluffy (NOTE: If you are using almond paste, make that first and add.)

Beat in eggs (one at a time), then blend in the vanilla and anise extract. In separate bowl, mix ground anise seeds, flour, baking powder, baking soda and salt. Add to butter, sugar and egg mixture and blend until smooth. Fold in nuts. Dough can be refrigerated, however, bring to room temperature before cooking. Divide the dough in half and shape on a lightly greased baking sheet (or one lined with parchment) into two 12 inch logs about 4 inches wide and   inch high. Place them 2 inches apart on sheet. I suggest using the light "double cookie sheet"' vs. the dark cookie sheet - the cookies bake more evenly and you won't get too much browning.

Bake in 350 degree oven for 25 minutes or until they are lightly puffed and browned. Cool for 10 minutes in the pan, then transfer to cutting board being careful to support the transfer of the whole cookie or it will break. Cut each log diagonally into inch slices. Place the slices cut side down on the baking sheet. Toast each side in a 275 degree oven for 10 minutes, until golden brown. Cool. Eat. Have fun!

ALMOND PASTE

Almond flavoring, a basic ingredient in traditional biscotti, is available commercially as a paste in tubes and jars and as a liquid extract. You can replace equal portions of sugar and almond paste in this recipe. The following yields   pound of almond paste which will keep for several months when stored in refrigerator. I have cut this in half when needed less and it worked well too. In food processor or blender, grind the almonds and sugar until very fine. Add the water, vanilla and almond extracts and blend until it is a paste- like consistency and forms into a ball. Remove, place on a board slightly dusted with powdered sugar, and roll into a one inch diameter log. Wrap in plastic wrap and refrigerate any amount left over from recipe.

Serving Ideas: I prefer the almonds whole in my biscotti, but you can chop them up - just don't chop too fine or you won't be able to taste the biscotti.

Chocolate Chip Cookies

Source: Alice Peters

Vicki's note: These are Alice Peters (Marshall's sister-in-law) famous chocolate chip cookies.... the ones she sends to me each year as a special treat that everyone else tries to hoard... the cookies that one year (at Thanksgiving) everyone else ate so I didn't get any... the ones I now don't tell anyone I have. They are great! I don't know if they will taste the same when you make them, but if they're not the best you've ever had, call Alice and maybe she'll whip you up a batch. I think it's her special touch that makes them taste so good!

1/3 cup Crisco

1/3 cup butter

1/2 cup sugar

1/4 cup brown sugar, packed

1 egg

1 teaspoon vanilla

1 1/2 cups flour

1/2 teaspoon baking soda

1/2 teaspoon salt

1/2 cup walnuts, chopped

6 ounces semisweet
chocolate chips

Heat oven to 375 degrees.

Mix together Crisco, butter and sugars until smooth. Beat in egg and vanilla on low speed about 1 to 2 minutes. In a separate bowl, mix flour (for a softer more rounded cookie, increase flour by 1/4 cup), baking soda and salt together. Mix dry ingredients into moist ingredients a little at a time until fully incorporated. Stir in nuts and chocolate chips.

Drop rounded teaspoonfuls of dough about 2 inches apart on an ungreased baking sheet. Bake 8 to 10 minutes or until delicately browned. Cookies should still be soft. They will crisp as they cool. Let cool slightly before removing from baking sheet and putting onto cooling rack.

Prep Time: 10 minutes   Start to Finish: 45 minutes   Servings: 48

Coconut Macaroons

Source: Peg Miller

Vicki's note: This recipe hales from my sister-in-law Peg - it was one of her mom's favorite cookie recipes.

2/3 cup all-purpose flour

5 1/2 cups shredded coconut

1/4 teaspoon salt

**1 14 oz. can sweetened
    condensed milk**

2 teaspoons vanilla

1/2 cup raisins, optional

Preheat oven to 350 degrees. Line cookie sheet with parchment or aluminum foil.

In a large bowl, stir together the flour, coconut and salt. Stir in the sweetened condensed milk and vanilla using your hands until well blended. Use an ice cream scoop to drop dough onto the prepared cookie sheets. Cookies should be about golf ball size.

Bake for 12 to 15 minutes in the preheated oven, until coconut is toasted. Remove immediately from pan to cooling rack.

Prep Time: 15 minutes   Start to Finish: 30 minutes   Servings: 25

Cucidati

Italian Fig Cookies
Source: Lucy Peters

Lucy's note: Italians traditionally make this cookie at Christmas time. Grandpa Amico (yes - Grandpa) used to enjoy making these. This recipe is a combination of Lucy Barone's and Aunt Sally's.

FILLING
1 pound dried figs
1/2 cup bourbon whiskey,
   or brandy
1 1/2 cups dried pitted dates
1 cup seedless raisins
1/2 cup honey
1/2 cup orange marmalade
Zest from 1 medium orange
Zest from 1 lemon
1/2 pound hazelnuts,
   toasted and chopped
1/2 pound almonds,
   toasted and chopped
1/2 teaspoon nutmeg
1 teaspoon cinnamon
1/2 cup orange juice
DOUGH
4 cups flour
3/4 cup sugar
4 teaspoons baking powder
1/2 teaspoon salt
1 cup butter
2 large eggs
1 tablespoon vanilla

1/2 cup milk
1 small egg, beaten slightly
   in small bowl (this is
   your "egg wash")
ICING
3 cups powdered sugar
1/4 cup warm water
1 tablespoon light corn syrup
1/4 teaspoon flavoring, lemon
   or orange work well
Confetti sprinkles

FILLING:

Make the filling ahead of time, as you need to let it rest for 8 hours to let the flavors meld. Warm brandy slightly, place figs in bowl with brandy and let "rest" for 1 hour. In food processor, combine the figs, dates and raisins and process to a medium fine chop. Add remaining filling ingredients (honey, orange marmalade, orange zest, lemon zest, hazelnuts, almonds, nutmeg, cinnamon and orange juice) and process until combined. Place in bowl, cover and refrigerate mixture for at least 8 hours.

DOUGH:

In a large bowl combine flour, sugar, baking powder and salt. Whisk to combine. Cut in butter (using a pastry blender or two knives) until mixture resembles coarse oatmeal. This can be done in electric mixer using dough hook but DO NOT over mix. In a separate bowl beat eggs, vanilla and milk together. Add to dry mixture and stir. Mix until dough is smooth. Form large ball, flatten a bit and cut into 4 pieces wrap in plastic wrap and refrigerate for 1 hour.

Pre-heat oven to 375 degrees, and lightly grease baking sheet with cooking spray or line with parchment. Turn each piece of dough out onto lightly floured board and roll into 12 inch square. Cut dough into 4" x 2" rectangles. Place 2 tablespoons of filling down center of each rectangle. Fold dough over (on long side) each rectangle to enclose filling; pinch edges to seal. Turn cookies over (seam-side down) and press gently to flatten the seams. NOTE: Be careful when handling cookie as filling can easily "poke through" dough which you don't want. Cut the logs crosswise into 1 1/2 to 2 inch-wide slices and arrange 1/2 inch apart on prepared baking sheets. Brush with egg wash. Bake 15 to 20 minutes, until golden brown. Remove from baking sheets and cool on wire racks.

ICING:

Place warm water in mixing bowl. Add syrup and flavoring. Mix to dissolve syrup. Add powdered sugar. Mix on low speed until a smooth glaze is formed. Glaze should be warm when placed on cookies. Warm in microwave for a few seconds if necessary. Store glaze in plastic container. No need to refrigerate. Glaze will stay for over a week.

Serving size: 100 cookies   Prep time: 1 hr.   Start to finish: 2 hr.

63

Ginger Snap Cookies

Source: Denise Bullock

Vicki's note: This recipe is from my sister-in-law Denise. Seems her kids like these crunchy, but Grandpa McNickle likes them soft. You may want to try two batches - one with the balls and one flattened and see which you prefer. I'm a crunchy cookie person myself!

3/4 cup shortening

1 cup sugar, plus 1/4 cup for rolling

1 egg

1/4 cup molasses

2 cups flour

3/4 teaspoon salt

1 teaspoon baking soda

1 teaspoon cinnamon

1 teaspoon cloves

1 teaspoon ground ginger

Preheat oven to 350 degrees.

In a large bowl combine shortening and sugar using an electric beater on medium speed. After shortening and sugar are a smooth but gritty consistency, add egg and beat until incorporated. Then beat in molasses.

In a separate medium bowl, combine flour, salt, baking soda and spices. Add dry mixture in batches to wet mixture, mixing to fully incorporate after each addition.

Put the remaining 1/4 cup sugar into a shallow bowl. Form dough into 1 inch balls, then roll each one lightly in sugar. Place 2 inches apart on an ungreased baking sheet that has been lined with parchment paper. Bake for 10 to 12 minutes, until cookies are light brown in color. Remove from oven, let cool for one minute, then place on a wire rack to cool completely.

NOTE: For a crunchier cookie, flatten each one slightly with the bottom of a drinking glass.

Prep Time: 15 minutes   Start to Finish: 30 minutes

Hello Dolly Bars

Source: Vicki McNickle

Vicki's note: This recipe was from a friend at Lifespring. Taylor discovered a way to improve on it when he made it in a 9" x13" pan one day, and ended up adding more nuts, chips and coconut, but leaving the condensed milk the same - they turned out perfect! This is now the revised recipe.

1/2 cup butter

1 1/2 cups graham cracker crumbs

1 1/2 cups walnuts, chopped

1 1/2 cups semisweet chocolate chips

1 1/2 cups flaked coconut

1 14 oz. can sweetened condensed milk

Preheat oven to 350 degrees. Spray sides and bottom of a 9" x 13" glass baking pan with cooking spray.

Melt butter. Mix into graham cracker crumbs. Press into bottom of pan. Sprinkle nuts, chocolate chips and coconut (in that order) over crust. DO NOT STIR! Pour condensed milk over all.

Bake at 350 degrees for 30 minutes. Allow to cool completely on wire rack (about 1 hour), then cut into 1 inch squares.

Prep Time: 10 minutes   Start to Finish: 45 minutes

Italian Almond Cookies

Source: Lucy Peters

Lucy's note: What would a holiday or Italian wedding be without these cookies! They are as much of a tradition as candy-covered almonds.

2 1/2 cups all-purpose flour

1 1/4 tablespoons baking powder

1/2 teaspoon salt

3 eggs, room temperature

2/3 cup sugar

8 tablespoons butter,
   room temperature

1 tablespoon shortening

1 teaspoon vanilla

1/2 teaspoon almond extract

1/4 cup milk, warm

ALMOND ICING

1 cup powdered sugar

1/2 teaspoon almond extract

2 tablespoons milk

Preheat oven to 350 degrees. Lightly grease a cookie sheet or line with parchment paper. Set aside.

In a medium mixing bowl stir together (with wire whisk) flour, baking powder and salt. Set aside. In bowl of electric mixer, slightly beat butter and shortening, add sugar and mix until creamed. Add room temperature eggs one at a time, beating until incorporated. Add vanilla and almond extracts and milk until combined. Add flour mixture a little at a time, beating after each addition just until incorporated. If dough becomes too stiff to continue beating in mixer, stir in any remaining flour by hand with a wooden spoon. Remove dough from bowl and form into ball. Wrap in plastic wrap and place in refrigerator for about 1 hour.

Remove dough from refrigerator. Roll into 1 inch balls and place on the prepared cookie sheet, 2 inches apart.

Bake for 10 to 12 minutes or until bottoms are lightly browned. Remove cookies from sheet and transfer to wire rack to cool. When they are cooled, ice with Almond Icing. May be sprinkled with colored sugar, if desired.

ALMOND ICING

Stir together powdered sugar, almond extract and milk and mix until icing is of spreading consistency. If too stiff, add very small amounts of milk little at a time. Icing can be made ahead and refrigerated while waiting for cookies to cool. Stir well with to get to spreadable consistency.

Prep Time: 35 minutes   Start to Finish: 1 hour 45 minutes

Italian Chocolate Cookies

Source: Lucy Peters

Vicki's note: Christmas would not be complete without these cookies! When I was a girl I loved making them with Mom, and as a Mom, I love making them with Taylor. I love the taste of them, I love the tradition of making them, and I love sharing them. They are a lot of work, but well worth the effort. This dough is very stiff and can be difficult to mix.

When I was a kid, Mom and I would switch off holding the pan and mixing. If you are not fortunate enough to have someone else to help, but do have a Cuisinart you can mix the dough in two batches using the dough blade. Another option is to use a sturdy mixer - this is what I use and it works great.

5 cups flour

3/4 teaspoon allspice

3/4 teaspoon cinnamon

3/4 teaspoon nutmeg

3/4 teaspoon cloves

8 tablespoons cocoa

5 teaspoons baking powder

1/2 cup butter, room temperature

1/4 cup Crisco, room temperature

1 1/4 cups sugar

1 tablespoon vanilla

1/2 10 oz. jar strawberry
  jam, 5 oz. total

1/2 cup coffee, strong

3 tablespoons bourbon whiskey

3/4 cup chopped dates

1/2 lemon, zested and juiced

1 orange, zested and juiced

2 cups toasted walnuts, chopped

1/2 cup chocolate chip

Icing - recipe for
  Cucidati cookies

In a very large bowl (using a large stock pot for mixing is sometimes easier) mix all dry ingredients through baking powder. Set aside

In another large bowl, mix sugar, butter and Crisco on low speed until well blended - about one minute. Then add remaining wet ingredients through orange. Mix well until all liquids are fully incorporated. Add dry ingredients to wet ingredients a cup at a time, until fully incorporated. Add chocolate chips and nuts and combine until incorporated using a wooden spoon or strong spatula. Dough will be thick and a little 'sticky. Chill dough thoroughly before baking (about 2 hours) in refrigerator covered with plastic wrap

Drop by rounded teaspoons onto ungreased or parchment lined cookie sheet and bake in pre-heated 350 degree oven for 8 to 10 minutes. If cookies are larger, you will need more cooking time. Chocolate continues to cook after removed from oven, so don't overcook. Cookies will be a bit soft when they come out and will harden as they cool.

Cookies can be stored in air-tight container in cool, dry place. Once cookies are completely cooled, ice with Cucidati icing recipe in book. This is best done just before serving as icing can make the cookie sticky when stored.

Kolache Cookies

Source: Carol Miller

Vicki's note: This is a recipe from my sister-in-law Carol which she got from her Grandma Ruth. Carol has a knack for baking wonderful tasting treats... now I know where she learned.
Carol's grandmother gave her original recipe cards many years ago that date back some sixty to seventy years!

8 cups flour, sifted

1 teaspoon salt

1 1/4 pounds margarine,
   or butter - softened

2 1/2 teaspoons active dry yeast

4 tablespoons sugar

2 1/2 cups milk, separate use

4 eggs, separated

4 pounds walnuts.,
   shelled and chopped

1/2 cup firmly packed
   brown sugar

1/2 cup granulated sugar

1/2 cup powdered sugar, sifted
   - for rolling out dough

CRUST: In a large bowl, blend together flour, salt, and margarine until mixed and pieces are the size of corn meal. Set aside.

In a cup, mix together yeast and sugar. Yeast will dissolve into sugar.

FILLING: In a separate bowl, beat egg yolks (NOTE: Reserve whites you will need them in a later step). and add 1 cup milk Add yeast mixture and stir together. Add liquid mixture to flour mixture and blend until smooth. Cover dough with plastic wrap and chill 4-6 hours or overnight.

Preheat oven to 325 degrees. Spread walnuts onto baking sheet and toast for 8 minutes. Let cool completely. Grind walnuts. Place walnuts in a bowl and add the 1/2 cup brown sugar, and 1/2 cup white sugar, stirring well to combine. The step can also be done in a food processor by placing all ingredients in processor and combining until nuts are ground. NOTE: Don't over grind nuts or they will turn to paste. In a separate bowl, beat reserved 4 egg whites until stiff, but not dry. Fold into nut and sugar mixture.

Scald 1 1/2 cups milk, let cool a bit and then pour over egg, sugar and nut mixture stirring gently until smooth.

In batches, place dough on pastry board that is lightly covered with sifted powdered sugar; roll out into 1/4 inch thickness. Cut rolled dough in 8 inch circles; spread circles with filling and cut each into 8 pie- shaped wedges. Roll up each wedge beginning at outside edge. Place cookies on cookie sheet that has been sprayed with cooking spray or been lined with parchment 1 1/2 inches apart. Bake in 325 degree oven for 12 to 15 minutes or until golden brown. Let cool completely. Cookies freeze very well in an airtight container.

Prep Time: 40 minutes   Start to Finish: 1 hour

Nut Bars

Source: Lucy Peters

Vicki's note: This is a great bar cookie to make at Christmastime. It is not too sweet, and is a simple yet delicious treat!

1/2 cup butter, room temperature

1 cup firmly packed brown sugar, divided use

1 cup flour

2 tablespoons flour

1/2 teaspoon baking powder

1/4 teaspoon salt

1 cup chopped walnuts

1/2 cup flaked coconut

2 eggs

1 teaspoon vanilla

1/4 cup granulated sugar

Preheat oven to 350 degrees.

Cream butter and 1/2 cup of the brown sugar. Slowly add 1 cup flour and mix on low speed; mixture will be lumpy. Pat down firmly into well-buttered 9" square pan (butter bottom and 1/2" up sides of pan), alternative is to use cooking spray, but butter will produce a better result. Bake crust at 350 degrees for 20 minutes.

In the meantime, mix 2 tbsp flour, baking powder, salt, nuts, and coconut; set aside. When crust is nearly baked, beat eggs and vanilla in a clean bowl just to blend. Add remaining 1/2 cup brown sugar and 1/4 cup granulated sugar a little at a time, beating until well blended. Fold in nut mixture. Pour over baked crust (don't worry if it is still hot) and return to oven. Bake an additional 20 minutes.

When slightly but not completely cooled, cut into squares. Sprinkle with powdered sugar just before serving.

Oatmeal Cookies

Source: Lucy Peters

Vicki's note: Mom used to make these when we were little - they are my favorite! They come out a bit crunchy outside and chewy inside - perfect!

3/4 cup shortening
1 cup brown sugar
1/2 cup white sugar
1 egg
1/4 cup water
1 teaspoon vanilla
1 cup flour
1/2 teaspoon salt
1/2 teaspoon baking soda
3 cups oats
1/3 cup raisins

Preheat oven to 350 degrees. Prepare cookie sheets, either by spraying with cooking spray or lining with parchment...

Cream shortening, brown sugar and white sugar in large bowl. Beat in eggs, water and vanilla. Set aside.

In a separate bowl, sift together flour, salt and baking soda. Add dry ingredients to liquid mixture, a little at a time mixing well. Stir in oats and raisins.

Drop by teaspoonful onto prepared cookie sheet 1 inch apart. Bake 12 to 15 minutes. Let sit on cookie sheet on top of a cooling rack for about 5 minutes, then gently remove from tray (see note). Let cool on rack completely. Cookies are done when just brown on the bottom - not burned! For variety, 1/2 cup chopped walnuts may be added as well.

Note: These cookies have a tendency to "fall apart"' when taking off the tray, so be careful. This goes away once they're cooled.

Prep Time: 15 minutes   Start to Finish: 30 minutes   Servings: 24

Old-fashioned Soft Pumpkin Cookies

Source: Alice Peters

Lucy's note: Another great contribution from Alice Peters.

2 1/2 cups flour

1 teaspoon baking powder

1 teaspoon baking soda

1/2 teaspoon salt

1 teaspoon ground cinnamon

1/2 teaspoon ground nutmeg

1/2 cup butter, softened

1 1/2 cups granulated sugar

1 cup canned pumpkin

1 egg

1 teaspoon vanilla

3/4 cup raisins

1/2 cup pecans, toasted

1 cup oatmeal

GLAZE

2 cups powdered sugar

3 tablespoons milk

1 tablespoon butter, melted

1 teaspoon vanilla

Preheat oven to 350 degrees.

In medium bowl, combine flour, baking powder, baking soda, salt, cinnamon and nutmeg; set aside.

In large mixing bowl, cream butter and sugar. Add egg and beat until incorporated. Add pumpkin and vanilla; beat until light and creamy. Add dry ingredients little at a time until complete incorporated. Stir in raisins, nuts and oatmeal.

Drop by rounded tablespoon onto greased or parchment lined cookie sheet 2 inches apart. Smooth tops of cookie with spatula. Bake in preheated 350 degree oven for 15 to 20 minutes, or until lightly browned. Cool on wire rack.

While cookies are baking, make glaze. Combine powdered sugar, milk, butter and vanilla. Blend until smooth.

Once cookies are completely cooled, drizzle with glaze, Glaze is optional and cookies can be served without it.

Sesame Seed Cookies

Source: Lucy Peters

Vicki's note: Making sesame seed cookies at Christmastime is an Italian tradition. There are many variations of this recipe. This particular version is from Mom.

3 cups all-purpose flour

3 teaspoons baking powder

1/4 teaspoon salt

1/4 cup vegetable shortening, such as Crisco

1/2 cup unsalted butter

1/2 cup powdered sugar

1/2 cup granulated sugar

2 large eggs, lightly beaten

1 1/2 teaspoons vanilla, or anise flavoring

1/2 cup milk

2 cups sesame seeds, lightly toasted

Preheat oven to 350 degrees.

Combine flour, baking powder and salt. Set aside.

Beat shortening and butter with electric mixer for about 30 seconds. Add powdered and granulated sugars; beat until fluffy. Add eggs one at a time then vanilla. Beat until combined. Add dry ingredients, a little at a time, mixing well after each addition. Do not overbeat dough as it will become tough. Remove dough from bowl, and form into ball. Cut into fourths, wrap in plastic wrap and refrigerate for about two hours.

On a lightly floured surface, working with one-fourth of dough at a time, roll pieces of dough into rope about 12 inch pieces. Roll in milk then sesame seeds and place on ungreased baking sheet about 1/4 inch apart. Bake on middle rack for 8 to 10 minutes. Cool on wire rack. Store in airtight container.

Prep Time: 20 minutes   Start to Finish: 3 hours 20 minutes

Sfinge

Italian Fried Sweet Breads
Source: Sally Tudini

Vicki's note: Aunt Sal tells me this was a traditional desert for Easter Sunday when she was growing up. They would take turns beating the eggs.

1 tablespoon butter, cubed

1 cup water

1 cup flour

1 pinch salt

4 large eggs

1 teaspoon vanilla

1 quart canola oil, for
    frying (or vegetable)

1 cup powdered sugar for dusting

1 cup honey, optional

Mix flour and salt in bowl - set aside. Bring butter and water to a boil. Add flour and salt mixture all at once stirring well. Remove from heat. Allow to cool for 5 minutes. Add eggs, one at a time, beating well after each addition. Stir in vanilla. Set aside and let rest for 20 minutes.

While dough is resting, heat oil in a heavy pot to 365 degrees (for best results use a thermometer for this).

Drop the batter by teaspoonful into hot oil. Do not crowd the dough pieces as they need room to expand. Fry until golden brown, Remove with slotted spoon and drain on paper towels. When cooled, sprinkle with powdered sugar or drizzle with honey. Let temperature come back up to 365 degrees before cooking next batch.

Prep Time: 1 hour

Surprise Cookies

Source: Carol Miller

Vicki's note: This recipe is from my sister-in-law Carol. She got it from her Grandma Ruth, who used to bake cookies by the gross when Carol was a girl.

1/2 cup shortening, such as Crisco

1 1/2 cups vegetable oil

1 cup sugar

6 cups flour, sifted, divided use

1 teaspoon baking soda

1 teaspoon salt

2 teaspoons baking powder

1/2 cup orange juice

1/2 cup milk

2 cups candied cherries, pitted date halves, and / or nutmeat, you can do a variety of fillings for cookies

SYRUP RECIPE:

2 cups water

1 cup honey

1 cup sugar

1 1/2 pounds walnuts, ground

DOUGH:

Preheat oven to 400 degrees. Prepare cookie sheets by spraying with cooking spray or lining with parchment paper.

Beat together shortening and sugar, then add oil and beat until fully incorporated. Set aside.

Sift together flour, baking soda, salt and baking powder. Mix 2 cups of dry mixture into shortening mixture. Stir in orange juice and milk. Gradually stir in remaining 4 additional cups of sifted flour (1 cup at a time) until the dough can be handled. If dough is too sticky add more flour a little bit at a time. Wrap dough in plastic wrap and refrigerate for 1 hour.

Remove dough from refrigerator. To form cookies, pinch off a small piece of dough, flatten in palm of hand and place a candied cherry, pitted date or nut meat in center. Roll into oblong, then gently roll on coarse side of cheese grater to perforate the dough. Place on prepared cookie sheets. Bake at 400 degrees for 10-12 minutes or until lightly browned. Cool on rack. When cool, dip in honey syrup (recipe below).

When all cookies have been baked and are cooling, reduce heat on oven to 325 degrees. Spread nuts onto a baking sheet, and bake for 8 minutes in 325 degree oven. When complete cooled, grind nuts. NOTE: Do not over grind or they will turn to a paste. You will want them to be coarse so you can roll honey-coated cookies in them. This step of cooking and grinding nuts can also be done ahead of time.

HONEY SYRUP:

Mix water, honey and 1 1/2 cup sugar in large heavy sauce pan. Bring to boil over low heat and continue to boil until mixture becomes the consistency of syrup. Dip cooled cookies into syrup one at a time using tongs or slotted spoon. Don't let cookies sit too long in syrup or they will get soggy. Lift out of syrup, drain off excess, then roll in ground walnuts, place on wire rack to cool completely and let syrup dry. Keep syrup at a slow simmer until all cookies are dipped. Cool completely and serve, or freeze. Store in airtight container, placing parchment or wax paper at bottom, between layers and on top.

Prep Time: 35 minutes   Start to Finish: 1 hour 30 minutes

Torcetti

An Italian "'biscuit" cookie
Source: Sally Tudini

Vicki's note: This recipe is from Aunt Sally Tudini, and as we all know, she makes awesome sweet treats! This recipe is originally from Grandpa Amico's mother, Salvatrice Palumbo Amico. Straight from the old country!

1/2 pound butter

1/2 pound shortening, Crisco

5 cups flour, sifted

1/2 cup milk, warm

1/2 teaspoon sugar

**1/2 teaspoon vanilla extract,
  or anise or almond**

1 package yeast, not quick rise

2 eggs, beaten

2 cups powdered sugar

In a large bowl, cut butter and shortening into flour until mixture is as fine as cornmeal. In a separate bowl combine milk, sugar and vanilla; stir in yeast until dissolved. Add yeast liquid to flour mixture. Add beaten egg. Mix until completely combined. Add more flour if too sticky. Knead slightly. Cover and place out of draft. Let stand until double in bulk (about 1 hour).

Heat oven to 375 degrees.

Sprinkle bread board with powdered sugar. Break off small pieces of dough, roll in sugar and create a rope ¼" round, and twist over in middle to create a loop. Place on greased baking sheet or one that has been lined with parchment paper and sprayed with cooking spray. Bake at 375 degrees for 12 to 15 minutes. Cookies should be golden brown. Cool completely.

Serving Ideas: Cookies can be stored in airtight container.

Prep Time: 30 minutes   Start to Finish: 1 hour 30 minutes

Back Row: David Amico, Johnathan Drost, Sallyanne Amico, Mike Amico, Paul Miller, Curt Amico, Len Amico, Len Miller, Harry Miller, Stephen Drost
Front Row: Lee Joe Amico, Diana Amico, Vicki McNickle, Cheryl Amico, Mathew Drost
Family Reunion, Buffalo NY in 2004

Lucy's middle son

Cooking is being Italian; being Italian is cooking...

Cooking is life. It causes me to focus in the moment. It causes me to be absorbed in all my physical senses. I smell the basil as I chop it. My eyes tear as I cut the onion; my ears are tickled by the sound of the knife on the cutting board.

Cooking is my escape from my head and into my body. Cooking is memories. It causes me to instantly be transported to my past. Eating or preparing food--cooking sauce, meatloaf, tasting biscotti, smelling coffee, scrambling eggs all are my time machine, transporting me to memories of voices, faces and events of my past. From Dad's browned scrambled eggs to having cereal with coffee and milk at Grandmas to discussions about stuffing at Thanksgivings, food has been at the center of the best moments of my life and continues to be so.

Cooking is my gift to my family, and I delight in watching them unwrap my gift to them. That is how I know I am Italian.

Desserts

Vicki, Lucy and Peg

Making Cannoli – our last time together making them

November 2010

Bread Pudding

Source: Sally Tudini

Vicki's note: I don't recall liking bread pudding much until I tasted Aunt Sally's. This is her own creation that she concocted when she had her own restaurant.

2 cups milk

1/2 cup sugar

2 cups white bread, crusts removed and then cubed (about 6 thick slices)

1/2 cup golden seedless raisins

5 eggs

1 teaspoon vanilla

Preheat oven to 350 degrees.

Scald milk in a large pan. Scalding milk means bringing it nearly to a boil, preferably in a thick-bottomed pan while stirring actively, to keep a protein skin from forming on the surface and to keep the proteins and sugar from sticking to the bottom.

While milk is heating, beat eggs and sugar together in a separate bowl. Once milk is scalded, add 1 cup to eggs and mix well, stirring constantly to avoid "cooking" the eggs. Turn off heat, and add remaining milk to eggs. Stir to mix completely. Add vanilla.

Meanwhile, cut bread into 1 inch cubes and place into a 9"x 9" glass baking dish that has been sprayed with cooking spray. Drizzle raisins over top.

Pour egg and milk mixture over bread - do not mix. Let liquids absorb into bread for about 10 to 15 minutes. Bake in a 350 degree oven for 40 to 45 minutes. Let cool before serving.

Cannoli
Italian Rolled Pastry
Source: Lucy Peters

Lucy's note: This recipe is from Aunt Gina's Mom (Mae Syracuse). The wine alterna-tive and lard alternative are from my lifelong friend, Lucy Barone. Both of these women knew & know Italian baking instinctively. Aunt Gina inherited her Mom's talent for great cooking!" Note from Vicki: This is the last thing I cooked with Mom. The day we rushed her to the hospital we had been making cannoli shells in the morning. It was a project we had been doing for years together the week before Thanksgiving. We made the final edits to this recipe that day.

CANNOLI SHELLS:
- 1 cup flour
- 1 tablespoon sugar
- 1 tablespoon vegetable shortening, or lard
- 1 egg yolk, beaten (save egg white)
- 1/4 cup bourbon whiskey (or red wine)
- 1 tablespoon vanilla
- water, lukewarm
- 1 quart corn oil, or canola oil

CANNOLI FILLING:
- 1 medium milk chocolate bar, with almonds
- 1 pound Ricotta Cheese
- 1/2 cup powdered sugar, plus extra for sprinkling on top of prepared shells
- 1/2 cup lightly toasted and chopped almonds
- 1/2 teaspoon cinnamon
- 1/2 pint whipping cream

CANNOLI SHELLS:

Shells take quite a while to make - it is a good idea to make these ahead of time (they store very well)

Mix flour and sugar together. Cut shortening into mixture (as for pie crust) until mixture resembles cornmeal consistency.

In separate bowl, mix egg yolk (reserve egg white), whis-key and vanilla. Add to flour mixture and mix until mix-ture has consistency of pie crust. If mixture seems too dry, add lukewarm water, a LITTLE at a time until proper consistency. Refrigerate dough covered tightly for mini-mum of 20 minutes. Can be refrigerated up to 7 days.

In the meantime, heat oil in deep fryer or in deep pan to about 375 degrees. You should definitely use a ther-mometer for this - having the oil hot enough is essen-tial for getting the perfect consistency for the shells. If the oil is not hot enough the shells will be too greasy.

Remove dough from refrigerator. Pinch off small piece of dough and roll out to about 1/8 inch thick sheets. If using Mixmaster with pasta attachment, take small piece of dough and starting at #1 - put through 2x, then #3 put through 2x, then #5 - put through 1x - this should get them to the right thickness. Cut into 4" x 4" square OR using a 4" round biscuit cutter or custard cup, cut out rounds. You can re-roll the cut off sides - but don't handle too much or dough will get tough. Wrap around cannoli form and seal with egg white (use your reserved egg white from above if you have it - beat slightly in a small bowl first). NOTE: Don't get the egg white on the form, or it will make the dough stick to the form, then you cannot get them off of the form - and that's when breakage happens! Good for snacking, no good for filling.

Deep fry 3 or 4 at a time until golden brown - it is very quick, so don't walk away! Remove cooked shells with tongs and place onto paper towels to cool, standing on end to let excess oil drip out. Using heavy duty pot holders or double folded kitchen towels, very carefully remove shells from forms using paper towels if necessary. NOTE: Be careful the form/pastry is cool enough to handle so you don't burn yourself, HOWEVER, remove from form fairly quickly after cooking so the pastry doesn't stick to the form. Make sure forms are cooled completely before putting on the next piece of dough.

Once completely cooled, shells can be stored in covered, airtight container for about a month, or filled if to be eaten right away. If they become soft, place in a 300 degree oven on a cookie sheet for about 3 to 5 minutes to crisp. JUST BEFORE SERVING, fill with cannoli filling. Enjoy!

CANNOLI FILLING

This should be made just a few hours AT THE MOST before serving in order to keep the whipping cream light and fluffy.

In preparation for making the whipped cream, place a 1 quart glass or metal bowl and beaters into the freezer while doing the next two steps.

Grate chocolate on the large holed side of a grater into medium bowl (can also be shredded in a small chopper if you have one). To this, add ricotta cheese, powdered sugar, chopped almonds and cinnamon. Combine well - the ricotta should not be lumpy and the powdered sugar should be fully incorporated. At this point you may want to taste the mixture and see if you want more sweetness, in which case, add more powdered sugar. We don't like this dessert too sweet in our family.

After about fifteen minutes, remove the quart bowl and beaters from the freezer, and beat the whipping cream until stiff peaks form. NOTE: Do not overbeat. Fold whipped cream into the ricotta mixture. If not serving immediately, keep mixture in refrigerator until ready to serve. Just before serving, fill each shell with about 2 rounded teaspoons of filling. Sprinkle tops with powdered sugar.

Prep Time: 1 hour   Start to Finish: 2 hours   Servings: 15

Cinnamon-scented Rice Pudding

Source: Vicki McNickle

Vicki's note: When I found this recipe I knew the best person to try it out on was my step dad, Marshall, as he loves rice pudding. Once it passed the test with him, I knew I had a sure way to soften him up in the future!

**3 1/2 cups 2% lowfat
   milk, divided**
**1/2 cup short grain
   rice, uncooked**
1/3 cup sugar
1 tablespoon margarin
lemon rind, 3 inch strip
1 cinnamon stick, 3 inches
1 egg
1 teaspoon vanilla extract
1/4 cup golden raisins, or regular

In a medium pot, combine 3 cups milk, uncooked rice, and next 4 ingredients. Bring milk / rice mixture to boil over medium-high heat. Reduce heat and simmer, uncovered for 10 minutes, stirring occasionally.

In a deep bowl, combine remaining 1/2 cup milk and egg, stirring with a wire whisk. Gradually stir about one- fourth of hot rice mixture into the egg mixture, stirring to combine. Add back to the rice mixture and stir well.

Reduce heat and simmer, uncovered, 40 minutes, stirring occasionally. Remove from heat; discard lemon rind and cinnamon stick. Stir in vanilla and raisins. Serve warm or chilled.

Prep Time: 5 minutes   Start to Finish: 1 hour   Servings: 6

Fudge

Source: Lucy Peters

Lucy's note: We used to make this at Christmastime when we lived in Buffalo and long before we all worried about "fat consumption". It's the easiest fudge to make and OH - SO DELICIOUS!

1/2 cup butter

1 12 oz. can evaporated milk

4 1/2 cups sugar

1/2 pound marshmallows, 35 count

2 ounces unsweetened chocolate

2 6 oz. packages semisweet chocolate chips

3 4 oz. packages dark sweet baking chocolate

1 tablespoon vanilla

2 cups chopped walnuts

In a large pot, combine butter, milk and sugar. Stir over medium heat until the sugar dissolves. Cook to a boil and cover. Boil for 5 minutes, then remove from heat.

Add marshmallows; stir until melted. Add the 3 kinds of chocolate (one at a time), stirring until melted. Add vanilla and nuts; blend well. Pour into an aluminum foil or parchment lined cookie sheet. Let stand until firm before cutting into squares.

Store in an airtight container with wax paper between layers.

Prep Time: 10 minutes   Start to Finish: 50 minutes

Lemon Ice

Source: Vicki McNickle

Vicki's note: I can remember going to Longo's ice cream stand in Buffalo, NY on hot summer nights as a kid and getting lemon ice in a paper cup. This recipe is from a newspaper and I have it on good word that it's pretty good!

1/2 cup water

3/4 cup sugar

3/4 cup lemon juice

1/4 teaspoon lemon zest, grated

1 dash salt

Mix together water, sugar, lemon juice, lemon zest and salt. Stir to dissolve sugar. Freeze in ice cream machine according to manufacturer's directions

Prep Time: 10 minutes   Servings: 8

Pumpkin Cheesecake

Source: Lucy Peters

Vicki's note: Mom has started making this for Thanksgiving each year, and it is delicious! She took up baking cakes and pies a lot more in these past few years after taking cake decorating classes. When we are all there, she really enjoys having an appreciative crowd to feed them to!

CRUST:

1 cup graham cracker crumbs,
   If using whole crackers,
   grind in food processor
   to make crumbs
3 tablespoons butter
2 tablespoons sugar

FILLING:

2 packages cream cheese (8 oz
   each), at room temperature
1 1/4 cups sugar
1 16 oz can canned pumpkin,
   NOTE: DO NOT use
   pumpkin pie filling
3/4 cup sour cream
2 tablespoons bourbon,
   or 2 tsp vanilla
1 teaspoon ground cinnamon
1/2 teaspoon allspice
3/4 teaspoon pumpkin pie spice
1/4 teaspoon salt
4 large eggs

SOUR CREAM TOPPING:

1 cup sour cream
3 tablespoons sugar
1 teaspoon vanilla extract

Preheat oven to 350 degrees. In small bowl stir graham cracker crumbs, melted butter and sugar until moistened. Empty into 9" x 3" spring form pan with hand press mixture into bottom of pan. Tightly wrap outside (bottom and sides) of pan with heavy-duty foil to prevent leakage when baking in water bath later. Bake crust 10 minutes. Cool completely in pan on wire rack.

Bring 2 quarts of water to boil for water bath. While crust bakes, prepare filling. In a large bowl, beat cream cheese on medium speed until smooth. With mixer running, add sugar gradually until blended, scraping sides as needed. With mixer at low speed, beat in pumpkin, sour cream, bourbon, cinnamon, allspice, pumpkin pie spice and salt. When fully blended, add eggs one at a time, beating until incorporated. Pour pumpkin mixture into cooled crust. Place pan in 2 inch deep roasting pan. Place pan on middle rack of oven. Carefully pour enough BOILING water into bottom of roasting pan to come one inch up side of spring form pan. About two quarts of water should be more than enough. Bake 1 hour and 10 minutes until the outside of the cheesecake sets but the center is still loose.

While cheesecake is cooking, prepare sour cream topping. In a small bowl beat sour cream, sugar and vanilla with wire whisk until blended.

When cheesecake is finished cooking, remove from water bath. Leave water bath in oven, and leave oven on. Spread sour cream topping over top of cheesecake, return to water bath in oven, and continue baking for 5 minutes.

Remove cheesecake from water bath to wire rack; remove foil. With small knife, loosen cheesecake from side of pan to help prevent cracking during cooling. Cool cheesecake completely. When cooled, cover and refrigerate at least six hours or overnight until well chilled. To serve, remove side of pan.

Prep Time: 35 minutes   Start to Finish: 2 hours   Servings: 16

Raspberry Walnut Shortbread Bars

Source: Carol Miller

Vicki's note: This recipe hails from Carol Miller. These treats are very good! Mom used to love them.

1 1/4 cups all-purpose flour

1/2 cup granulated sugar

1/2 cup cold butter, cut
    into tablespoons

1/3 cup seedless red
    raspberry jam

2 eggs

1/2 cup brown sugar,
    firmly packed

1 teaspoon vanilla

2 tablespoons flour

1/8 teaspoon salt

1/8 teaspoon baking soda

1 cup chopped walnuts

Preheat oven to 350 degrees

SHORTBREAD:

Combine 1 1/4 cups flour and granulated sugar. Cut in butter until mixture is like fine cornmeal. Press into bottom of lightly greased 9 inch square baking pan to make an even layer. Bake in 350 degree oven for 20 to 25 minutes, or until edges become lightly golden.

TOPPING:

While shortbread is cooking, mix together the topping. Beat eggs with brown sugar and vanilla until well blended. In a small bowl mix together 2 tablespoons of flour with salt and soda. Beat into egg and sugar mixture until blended. Stir in walnuts

When bottom is finished, remove from oven and spread raspberry jam over shortbread. Top with the egg / brown sugar and walnut mixture.

Return to oven and bake 20 to 25 minutes longer or until top is set. Cool in pan, and then cut into bars.

Prep Time: 15 minutes   Start to Finish: 55 minutes

Strawberries a La Marnier

Source: Vicki McNickle

Vicki's note: Mom got the recipe from the Chef at the La Costa Resort and Spa in the late 70's (while dining at Pisces Restaurant with Marsh).

4 tablespoons heavy cream, other whipped topping

4 tablespoons sour cream

2 tablespoons brown sugar

1/2 tablespoon Grand Marnier

2 tablespoons dark rum

1 pint strawberries, cleaned and dried

Whip heavy cream in cold non-metal bowl. When stiff peaks have formed, whip in sour cream and brown sugar. Stir in Grand Marnier and rum.

Clean strawberries, let dry on paper towels. Place strawberries on platter with cream dipping sauce. Enjoy!

Serving Ideas: This is a small batch, but you can always double or triple it. This is a very fun, easy and delicious recipe to serve when you have company. I have experimented with Kahlua in place of the Grand Marnier and it is as delicious.

Prep Time: 15 minutes   Servings: 4

Struffoli

Vicki's note: Aunt Sally tells me this recipe is originally from Grandma Amico's grandmother, Marianna Guido. I recall Mom making these when we were kids. Traditionally, these are served at St. Joseph Day tables and at Easter.

1 tablespoon butter, softened

1/4 cup sugar

4 large eggs

1 teaspoon vanilla

1 teaspoon cinnamon

2 1/2 cups flour

1 cup canola oil, or vegetable oil

1/2 cup honey

In a large bowl, mix together butter and sugar. Once well combined, add eggs one at a time, incorporating each one completely before adding next. Add vanilla and cinnamon - mix until blended. Add flour, 1 cup at a time. Dough should be smooth. If necessary, add more flour to smooth. Cover dough with a dish towel (in bowl) and allow to rest for about 1/2 hour at room temperature (out of drafts).

In a large pot, heat oil to 365 degrees (best to use a thermometer for this). While oil is heating, roll out dough into "logs" on lightly floured surface, 1/2 inch wide and about a foot long. Cut into 1/2 inch pieces. Carefully drop the pieces of dough into the hot oil, a handful at a time. When golden brown, remove from oil with a slotted spoon and place on paper towels to drain.

Heat honey to just under boiling point. Place cooled Struffoli in a bowl and drizzle with the warm honey. Gently toss. Arrange on large platter and sprinkle with colored sprinkles. Shape into a pyramid-like mound or into a wreath shape on a large plate. These little sweet treats are better the same day they're made, as they lose their crispness rather quickly. If you would like to save some for another day, do not drizzle with honey. Store in an airtight container. They can be crisped in a 250 degree oven for about 3 or 4 minutes. Remove from oven and proceed with honey and sprinkles.

Prep Time: 50 minutes   Start to Finish: 1 hour 20 minutes

Zabaglione and Strawberries
Italian Sweet Custard with Strawberries
Source: Sally Tudini

Vicki's note: Another great from Aunt Sal! This is originally from Grandma Amico's mother, Rosaria Vaccalluzzo. It's a Northern Italian recipe. This was a special dish served on holidays.

3 egg yolks

3 teaspoons sugar

1/4 cup Marsala wine

Pinch salt

1 1/2 pints strawberries

About 20 minutes before serving, wash, dry and hull strawberries. If they are very large, cut in half. Arrange berries in 4 wine goblets or desert dishes, set aside.

Bring 1-inch of water to a boil in a 4-quart saucepan set over high heat.

Add the egg yolks and sugar to a large glass bowl. Using an electric hand mixer on the highest speed, beat the eggs and sugar until the mixture is thick, pale yellow, and the sugar is completely dissolved, 4 to 5 minutes. Decrease the mixer speed to low and add the Marsala and salt.

Decrease the heat to maintain a simmer and put the bowl atop the saucepan with the boiling water, making sure the bottom of the bowl is not touching the water. Beat the mixture on medium speed, until it is thick, frothy, holds a ribbon, and when a spoon of mixture is dropped in pan it leaves a slight mound.

Spoon the warm mixture into custard cups over strawberries and serve immediately or allow to cool slightly.

Serving Ideas: This is great with any berries, pears or peaches as well.

Prep Time: 15 minutes   Start to Finish: 35 minutes   Servings: 4

Jordan Miller (left) Born Dec 2010 and her baby sister Skyler (right) born Aug, 2014
Jason & Liz Miller's daughters

Lucy's youngest son

Food is love and love is food!

When my daughter's friends walk through my door, they know that it is best if they have fasted for at least six hours before coming to Dad's. When Jason comes home with his family, he says, "Your house and Grandma's house always smell so good!"

It's always been about the food. Grandpa Amico with his wheeled cart carefully selecting the ingredients for the meal. He walks to the bakery in the winter with my little sister to feast on fresh hot rolls. There are buffalo pizza and wings with pitchers of soda pop at Uncle Angelo's. The smell of meatballs are frying in Aunt Sally's kitchen. There were cardoon and any other weed we could batter and deep fry or coat in olive oil and garlic. Every holiday, birthday, celebration or tragedy is marked with the breaking of bread and a shot of tequila!

Want proof that food is love just look at the Cannoli recipe! Mom would make the dough, roll it out, cut it, fry it and that is just the shell. Then comes the filling, chopping nuts and chocolate, stuffing the shells, more grated chocolate and sifted powdered sugar! HOURS! Devoured in minutes (ok...seconds)!

Love is my mother's hands cooking. Love is my mother's beautiful face leaning over a pot of sauce, smelling for the right combination while we crowd around with hunks of bread for the taste test. Love is talking to my mother on the phone on a Sunday afternoon to get the ingredients right for a recipe, cradling the phone between ear and shoulder while chopping and stirring.

I judge a home by the kitchen's proximity to the family room and how many butts will fit in it at a family gathering because everybody in our family cooks, helps and cleans up.

God bless you all!

The joy and memories contained in these pages are the story of our family's love and peace.

Lunch

Len, Paul, Vicki, Paul Sr. and Harry
Mid 90's

Fluffer Nutter Sandwich

Source: Paul Miller, Sr.

Vicki's note: When I got this sandwich for lunch as a kid, I knew I'd done something right! This gooey, chewy and delicious treat has now become a favorite of Taylor's. It's always fun to introduce this to the kid's friends who have never tried it before.

2 slices bread

3 tablespoons peanut
   butter, creamy or crunchy
   - whatever you prefer

3 tablespoons marshmallow
   cream, aka marshmallow fluff

Place peanut butter and fluff between slices of bread, pour yourself a very large glass of milk and chow down!

Prep Time: 3 minutes   Servings: 1

Leonard and Marianne Amico

Early 1960's

Note from Vicki: This is how I remember my grandmother and grandfather –

soft, sweet and cuddly!

Meats

Angelo Amico, Joe Amico, Marianna Drost, Marianne Amico, Lucy Peters

Buffalo, NY

Taken in late 90's or early '00's

Braciole

Stuffed meat rolls that
are cooked in marinara sauce
Source: Lucy Peters

Vicki's note: Mom used to help Grandma make these. As now, they were made only on special holidays or occasions. Aunt Mary Ann Amico made many of these for Uncle Sam. He loved his braciole. He particularly enjoyed the sliced braciole as a cold sandwich. NOTE: These are added to sauce at start of cooking.

6 slices flank steak (about 6" x 6" pieces) 1/8" thick (ask butcher to slice for you)

2 cups meatball mixture (look at recipe in book)

4 eggs, hard-boiled, and sliced lengthwise

3/4 medium red onion, sliced 1/4", rings separated

1/2 pound Italian salami (about 12 slices)

1/2 pound capicola (about 12 slices)

6 tablespoons Romano cheese, grated

1 1/2 teaspoons dried basil

8 feet kitchen string, for securing your rolls

Pot spaghetti sauce, see recipe in book - uncooked

Pound flank steak slightly with meat tenderizer. To prepare each roll: Spread 1/3 cup meatball mixture over each slice - making sure to leave 1/2 inch clear around all edges while filling. Layer in 3 slices red onion, 1/8 teaspoon basil, 1 Tbsp. Romano cheese, 4 slices egg, 2 slices salami, and 2 slices capicola. Roll up (from long side), tucking in filling as you roll. Tie ends and middle of roll with kitchen string. .

Brown either side in sauté pan about 5 minutes per side or in 350 degree oven for about ten minutes. Add to uncooked spaghetti sauce. Simmer in the sauce (over low heat) for about 2 to 2 1/2 hours.

Simmering over low the heat allows the meat to become tender. Remove from sauce, cover with aluminum foil and let rest for about 20 minutes before slicing. Remove string and slice to whatever thickness you desire, cover with sauce, sprinkle a bit more Romano cheese and enjoy along a plate of spaghetti, or manicotti, or ravioli. Cold, the braciole makes a wonderful sandwich next day.

Prep Time: 1 hour   Servings: 12

Carnitas

Mexican Pulled Pork

Source: Paul Miller, Jr.

Vicki's note: This recipe is from my brother Paul. He is known for his great Mexican food, and this recipe is a big hit at his house!

5 pounds Pork Shoulder, or
   Butt Roast

5 cloves garlic

2 large onion

2 large carrots, peeled

2 jalapenos, seeded and diced

1 cup fresh cilantro

1 tablespoon salt

1/2 tablespoon peppercorn

1 lime

2 tablespoons Emeril's Essence
   (you can find it in the grocery
   store or look up recipe at
   foodnetwork.com)

1/2 teaspoon oregano

In a large pot, cover pork with cold water to just about 1/2 inch above meat. Cut onion into quarters, lime in half, carrot in half, and jalapeno peppers (make sure to discard the seeds) in half - put all of this plus the peeled garlic into the pot with the pork. Add spices and stir. Bring water to a boil on high heat, then reduce heat, cover pot and simmer for 3/12 to 4 hours, stirring occasionally.

When pork is almost finished cooking on stove, turn on oven to 425 degrees. When pork is done, remove from pot (don't throw away liquid) and put in large foil lined roasting pan. Place pork in pre-heated oven for 20 to 25 minutes, uncovered.

While roast is in oven, strain the broth reserving the liquid.

Remove pork to a large cutting board, and shred with two forks. Put into a large serving dish, and pour about 1 1/2 cups of the cooking liquid over the meat.

Serve with tortillas, rice, beans and salsa.

Prep Time: 15 minutes   Start to Finish: 4 hours 30 minutes   Servings: 10

Grilled Leg of Lamb

Source: Paul Miller, Jr.

Vicki's note: My brother Paul is a great cook. This recipe has a reputation that spans the whole United States I'm pretty sure. This recipe is originally from his Pal Dale

5 pounds leg of lamb

1/4 cup olive oil

6 cloves garlic, crushed

1 teaspoon pepper

10 fresh limes (divided use)

4 cups pickled jalapeno juice, from canned (divided use)

Filet lamb from bone to create a flat roast (or purchase boneless leg of lamb). Remove extra fat and skin from meat.

In a small mixing bowl mix together olive oil, crushed garlic, juice from 3 limes, 1 cup (approximately) jalapeno juice and crushed black pepper. Rub well into meat and place in large zip-lock bag with remaining Refrigerate overnight. It's a good idea to put plastic bag in a container; that way if it gets a hole, it won't drip all over your fridge.

About 1/2 hour before getting ready to grill meat, turn on grill to medium to heat up, and take meat out of fridge to warm up a bit.

Remove lamb from bag and place on grill over medium heat for 30 to 40 minutes, basting with remaining lime juice and jalapeno juice, turning several times during cooking. Outside should be crispy, center slightly pink when done.

Prep Time: 40 minutes   Start to Finish: 1 hour 15 minutes   Servings: 6

Irene's Meatloaf

Source: Irene Amico

Lucy's note: This recipe is from Irene (Walsh) Amico, who is my brother Angelo's wife. This is her special version of meatloaf - very yummy!

1 small onion, finely chopped
  and cooked to translucent

1 pounds ground beef

2 eggs

1/2 cup Italian breadcrumbs

1/4 cup Romano cheese, grated

1 cup tomato sauce

1/2 tsp. salt

1/4 tsp. pepper

3 tablespoons barbeque sauce

1/2 cup grated mozzarella cheese

Preheat oven to 350 degrees. Prepare loaf pan by spraying with vegetable spray. Set aside.

Combine meat with cooked and cooled onion in large bowl. Add 2 eggs, breadcrumbs and Romano cheese. Add tomato sauce in increments, combining thoroughly after each addition. If mixture seems to be getting too moist, do not add full amount of sauce. Stir in salt and pepper to taste. Place 1/2 of mixture into prepared loaf pan. Cover with shredded mozzarella. Cover with second half of meat mixture. A light coating of barbecue sauce may be brushed on top of loaf, if desired.

Bake for 45 to 60 minutes. Allow to sit covered for about 10 minutes after removing from oven before slicing.

Serving Ideas: Serve with mashed potatoes and a green salad.

Prep Time: 20 minutes   Start to Finish: 1 hour 10 minutes   Servings: 6

Liver & Onions

Source: Vicki McNickle

Vicki's note: This recipe is from Grandma Amico. As a kid, I was one of the few in my house besides Mom who liked liver. For that reason, it was not served often, but when it was... mamma. When I was about 18 my friend May Tucker, introduced me to liver with onions and apples...I didn't think liver and onions could get better, but it did.

3 tablespoons butter

3 tablespoons olive oil

2 onions, very thinly sliced

1 Granny Smith apple, sliced thin (optional)

1/4 cup flour

1 tablespoon parsley

Salt and freshly ground pepper

1 pound fresh calf's liver

1/2 cup milk

1/3 cup red wine

Pinch sugar

1/8 cup balsamic vinegar

Heat 2/3 of the butter and olive oil in a large heavy skillet, add the onions and cook over low heat for about 40 minutes. If using apples, add 1/2 way through. When the onions are soft and golden remove to a serving dish and keep warm.

While onions are simmering, mix flour, parsley, salt and pepper in bowl. Dip liver in milk then coat in flour mixture. Let sit for about 10 minutes.

Heat remaining butter and olive oil in the skillet over medium heat. When the butter / olive oil mixture begins to foam add the liver and cook for about 3 minutes on each side: do not overcook. Remove the liver to the serving dish with the onions and keep warm. Add the wine and sugar to the pan juices and heat through. When slightly reduced, pour over the liver and serve. When liver and onions are served on the individual plates; drizzle a small amount of the balsamic vinegar over the dish.

Serving Ideas: You can use the apples in this recipe or leave out - they will make it a bit sweeter. Use good balsamic vinegar in this dish if possible - it will add a very rich flavor.

Prep Time: 20 minutes   Start to Finish: 40 minutes   Servings: 4

Meatballs

Source: Lucy Peters

Vicki's note: Mom's meatballs are one of a kind! You cannot find meatballs like this in a restaurant. The three meats, cheese and moisture are part of what makes them unique.

Lucy's note: Aunt Rosie used to make "Surprise Meatballs" which were to "die for". Following is her method:

Hard boil some eggs; cool and cut in half or thirds; wrap meatball mixture around each egg piece; proceed with directions below.

1 pound ground beef, no
   more than 7% fat

1/2 pound ground veal

1/2 pound ground pork

1 medium onion, finely chopped

2 cloves garlic, minced

3 eggs

1 cup Italian bread
   crumbs, flavored

3/4 cup Romano cheese, grated

1 teaspoon Salt

1/2 teaspoon Pepper

6 tablespoons fresh parsley,
   or 3 tablespoons dried

1/2 cup water, Add up to 1/4
   cup more - consistency
   should be moist

Chop onion and garlic. Sauté onions until translucent, 8-10 minutes. Add garlic and sauté one more minute. Set aside in blow to cool. In a large bowl, mix remaining ingredients, adding onion and garlic once cooled. The consistency should be very moist, but not "mushy." Add more cold water, a little at a time, if needed. Shape into 3 inch balls and broil for about 4 minutes on each side. Add to sauce about 45 minutes before serving time to let them finish cooking. If you are not going to finish cooking in sauce, then extend cooking time to 8 minutes per side under broiler.

See spaghetti sauce recipe for sauce.

Serving Ideas: (Vicki's note :) In the last few years I've started to sauté my onions and garlic before mixing with meat so as to 'mellow out" the flavors of the onion and garlic a bit. I left this recipe as it was passed down to me – you may try the sautéed onions if you find that you get heartburn from meatballs as I did.

These freeze very well. I suggest you freeze them separate from sauce in a plastic freezer bag so you can heat them up easily for sandwiches, and so the sauce will defrost faster as well.

Prep Time: 30 minutes   Start to Finish: 45 minutes   Servings: 18

Lucy's Meatloaf

Source: Lucy Peters / Vicki McNickle

Lucy's note: This is one of Len's childhood favorites! My sister Rosie would put hard- boiled egg slices in the middle of the meatloaf by putting half the meat mixture in pan, then adding 2 sliced hardboiled eggs, then topping with remaining meat.

Vicki's note: I added the topping on this recipe later and my family loves it.

3/4 pound lean ground beef

3/4 pound ground pork

2 eggs, slightly beaten

1 teaspoon salt

1/2 teaspoon pepper

1 cup plain bread crumbs, or
   Italian seasoned bread crumbs

1 small onion, finely chopped

1 cup tomato sauce

1 teaspoon Worcestershire
   sauce, divided use

few drops Tabasco
   sauce (optional)

2 tablespoons ketchup

2 teaspoons prepared mustard

Preheat oven to 350 degrees. Spray loaf pan lightly with vegetable spray. Set aside.

Combine beef and pork together in large bowl. Add eggs, salt, pepper, breadcrumbs, onion and mix well. Add tomato sauce in increments, combining thoroughly after each addition. Try not to make mixture too moist. Mix in 1/2 teaspoon Worcestershire sauce and Tabasco sauce (if using). Place meat in loaf pan.

In a small bowl mix together the ketchup, mustard and 1/2 teaspoon Worcestershire sauce. Spread over top of meatloaf.

Bake at 350 degrees for 45 to 60 minutes. Allow to set for 10 minutes before slicing.

Serving Ideas (Lucy's Note): Hard boil two eggs. Place one half of prepared meat mixture into pan. Slice and place hardboiled eggs on top. Cover with remaining meat mixture. Bake as directed.

Prep Time: 15 minutes   Start to Finish: 1 hour   Servings: 8

Ossobucco

Source: Lucy Peters

Vicki's note: I think you could survey my brothers and would find this is one of their favorite things to eat! Strangely enough - it was the meal Paul was making the night Mom passed away. We all came back to the house afterwards and ate it - knowing Mom would be happy we were eating one of the dishes she so loved to make for her kids! She was with us at the table that night - we all felt it.

4 large veal shank crosscuts

1 cup flour

1/3 cup olive oil, divided use

1 teaspoon salt

1/2 teaspoon pepper

1 16 ounce can beef broth

1 onion, chopped

2 cloves garlic, crushed

3 medium carrots, sliced

1 leek, sliced

3 medium celery stalks

3 whole cloves

2 bay leaves

1/2 teaspoon sage

1/2 teaspoon thyme

1/2 teaspoon parsley

1/2 cup red wine

1 28 ounce can crushed tomatoes

1 tablespoon grated lemon peel

Dredge veal crosscuts with flour. Heat several tablespoons of olive oil in a large skillet. Brown the veal well, season with salt and pepper, and transfer to a large pot or Dutch oven. Handle gently so the marrow remains in the bones. Once all veal shanks are browned and in the casserole, pour in the beef broth.

In a medium pot heat 3 tablespoons of oil on medium heat. When the oil is hot, sauté the onion, garlic, carrot, leek and celery over medium heat for about 5 minutes. Stir in the cloves, bay leaf, sage, thyme and parsley. Pour in the wine and continue cooking until the wine is almost evaporated about 10 minutes. Stir in the crushed tomatoes and lemon peel. Cook over medium heat for 10 minutes.

Pour tomato mixture over the meat in large pan or casserole dish. Cover tightly and simmer for 1 1/2 hours, or until meat is tender. Remove veal to serving dish and keep hot.

Force the vegetables and juice from the casserole dish through a sieve or food mill. If the resulting sauce is thin, cook over high heat to reduce liquid. Season sauce if necessary with salt and pepper. Pour sauce over meat to serve.

Prep Time: 30 minutes   Start to Finish: 2 hours   Servings: 4

Pork Roast with Vegetables

Source: Alan Cooper

Vicki's note: This recipe is from our friend Alan Cooper - it's always a hit with Kari, Kelsey, and Taylor.

2 tablespoons vegetable oil

2 pounds pork loin, center cut

4 tablespoons butter, divided use

2 medium onions, sliced 1" thick

1 head fennel, core and top removed, and sliced 1" thick

4 carrots, peeled and sliced 1" thick

4 stalks celery, sliced 1" thick

3 cloves garlic, peeled and smashed

1 teaspoon salt

1/2 teaspoon pepper

3 sprigs thyme

3 sprigs rosemary

2 apples (Roma or Red Delicious) cored and peeled and cut into 8 slices

2 tablespoons apple cider vinegar

1 cup apple cider

2 tablespoons whole grain mustard

Heat oil in large oven proof skillet on medium high heat, sear pork loin on all sides until browned. Remove meat from pan and set aside. Heat oven to 400 degrees

In same pan (do not clean out) melt 2 tablespoons of butter on medium heat. Add onion, fennel, carrots, celery and garlic. Sauté until lightly browned, about 10 to 15 minutes. Add salt, pepper, thyme, rosemary and apples - toss together with vegetables.

Return pork back to pan and surround with vegetables. Place in 400 degree oven and cook until meat temperature (using a meat thermometer) reaches 140 degrees - about 35 to 40 minutes.

Remove pan from oven, and put meat on a platter - cover lightly with aluminum foil and let rest for ten minutes. Put vegetables in covered serving dish to keep warm.

Put skillet back on stove, add cider vinegar and cook until reduced by 1/2. Add 1 cup apple cider and cook 5 more minutes until warm. Take skillet off heat, whisk in remaining 2 tablespoons butter and whole grain mustard, heat briefly then turn off heat.

Remove the strings from the roast and slice into 1/2-inch thick pieces and arrange over the apple mixture on a platter.

Drizzle some sauce over meat and serve the rest on the side.

Serving Ideas: This is great served with mashed potatoes on the side.

Prep Time: 30 minutes   Start to Finish: 1 hour 15 minutes   Servings: 6

Potatoes, Sausage and Peppers

Source: Vicki McNickle

Vicki's note: This recipe has become a traditional dish we prepare when we're all together at Thanksgiving. The biggest fans of this dish remain to be the Giglio family, however. Whenever I go to visit them it is on the list of "Vicki has to make" dishes... Makes me very happy!

4 tablespoons olive oil, divided use

5 links Italian sausage, sweet or Sicilian style

2 large potato, washed, peeled, cut into 1" cubes

1 medium green bell pepper, cored, seeded and cut into 1" pieces

1 large yellow onion, chopped

5 pepperoncini, stemmed, seeded and chopped

1 1/2 teaspoons salt

1/2 teaspoon pepper

1/2 teaspoon crushed red pepper

Cut sausage links into bite-sized pieces. Heat a large 12" pan over medium high heat, add 1 tablespoon olive oil. Heat briefly, then add sausage and cook until browned on all sides - about 15 minutes. When cooked, drain on paper towel lined plate. Set aside.

While sausage is cooking, place potato cubes in large microwave safe bowl. Add 1/4 cup of water, cover with plastic wrap, leaving a place for steam to vent on one side. Microwave potatoes for 5 to 8 minutes. You want them cooked but still a little firm. Fork should be easily inserted into potatoes but they should not be overly soft or mushy.

In the same pan, heat 2 tsp oil and then add onion and bell peppers. Cook for about 8 to 10 minutes on medium until the onions are slightly browned. Onions and bell peppers should be completely cooked and soft - if not, cook longer. Remove onions and peppers to a separate bowl.

Increase heat to medium high, add final tablespoon of oil. Add potatoes and fry until browned on all sides - 8 to 10 minutes. Return sausage back to pan along with onions, bell peppers, and pepperoncini, salt, pepper, and red pepper flakes. Stir to mix. Continue cooking 10 minutes on medium low heat to allow flavors to meld.

Serving Ideas: This is very tasty with Italian bread and a side salad.

Prep Time: 30 minutes   Start to Finish: 1 hour 15 minutes

Shepherd's Pie

Source: Astrid Amico

3 medium potatoes, peeled and
  chopped into small chunks
1 tablespoon oil
1 pound ground beef, or
  beef and lamb mixture
2 cloves garlic, minced
2 parsnips, minced
1 medium onion, minced
3 carrots, minced
1 cup beef broth
4 teaspoons cornstarch
1 teaspoon Worcestershire sauce
1/2 teaspoon hot sauce, optional
1 tablespoon salt
1/2 teaspoon pepper
4 tablespoons cheddar cheese,
  grated (or Swiss cheese)

Pre-heat oven to 400 degrees.

Place potatoes in large pot and add enough cold water to cover the potatoes. Cook 13 to 15 minutes or until very tender. While potatoes are cooking, dice the onions, carrots and parsnips and cook in the microwave on high for 2 to 4 minutes until softened (not mushy).

Heat oil in a skillet. Add garlic and sauté for about 1 minute. Add ground meat and cook through - 8 to 10 minutes.

While the meat is cooking dissolve the corn starch into 1 cup of beef broth stirring with fork to incorporate; set aside. Once meat mixture is cooked add the softened vegetables to the skillet with the meat. Pour cornstarch and beef broth mixture over the ground beef and vegetables and stir on low heat until slightly thickened. Season with Worcestershire sauce, hot sauce, salt and pepper. Simmer for 10 more minutes, stirring often.

While meat and veggies are simmering, drain the cooked potatoes and mash with butter, salt and pepper until smooth.

Pour meat mixture into the bottom of an 8" round and 4" deep casserole dish that has been sprayed with cooking spray. Smooth the mashed potatoes over the meat and vegetables, and sprinkle grated cheese over the top.

Bake at 400 degrees for 15 minutes. Cover and let set for five minutes before serving.

Serving Ideas: Astrid says that true Shepherd's pie is all ground lamb, but the flavor is very strong so it is often mixed with beef. An all beef pie is called "Cottage Pie" in England.

Prep Time: 45 minutes   Start to Finish: 1 hour 5 minutes   Servings: 4

Stuffed Pork Chops

Source: Lucy Peters

Vicki's note: I remember Mom making these when I was a kid - and I loved them! Next to Mom's pork roast and mashed potatoes with gravy, this is the next best way to eat pork.

4 pork chops, 2" thick

2 tablespoons butter

1/4 onion, chopped fine

2 slices thick bread, day old

2 tablespoons Romano cheese

1 tablespoon dried parsley

1/4 teaspoon poultry seasoning

1/8 cup chicken broth

1/2 teaspoon salt

1/4 teaspoon pepper

Preheat oven to 350 degrees.

Using a sharp knife with a long blade, cu a slit in side of pork chop - making a "pocket" for stuffing. Set aside.

Melt butter in a skillet over medium heat. Sauté onion until translucent (about 5 to 8 minutes) and remove from heat. Cube bread into small chunks, and add remaining ingredients. Mixture should be the consistency of thick stuffing. If more liquid is necessary additional chicken broth can be added.

Stuff pork chops with mixture and secure with toothpicks. Salt and pepper both sides of pork chops. Place on lightly greased baking sheet (or bottom half of broiler pan) and cook for 25 minutes in 350 degree oven. Remove from oven and cover with aluminum foil. Let rest for 10 minutes before serving.

Serving Ideas: I recently learned a little trick from a friend that putting pork (or any meat) in a bath of cider vinegar for 30 minutes before cooking allows the meat to tenderize and makes it more juicy. If you have the time, you might want to try this. Rinse and dry off meat before proceeding with the recipe as called for here.

Serve with mashed potatoes and spinach as side dishes.

Prep Time: 30 minutes   Start to Finish: 1 hour   Servings: 4

Swiss Steak

Source: Sandy Amico

Vicki's note: We received this recipe from Len Amico, who got it from his Mom, Sandy Amico.

2 tablespoons flour

1/2 teaspoon salt

1/4 teaspoon pepper

1/2 cup milk

1 1/2 pounds round steak,
   pounded and cut into
   4 serving pieces

1 tablespoon olive oil

1 large green bell pepper,
   cored, seeded and sliced

1 medium onion, sliced 1/4" thick

1 clove garlic, minced fine

1 15 oz. can diced tomatoes

1 cup water

Combine flour, salt and pepper in a shallow bowl. Pour milk in another shallow bowl. Wipe steaks dry with paper towels, dip into milk, then dredge in flour mixture; put on plate.

Heat olive oil in large frying pan over medium heat. Place steaks in hot oil, brown on both sides - about 2 minutes a side. Remove from pan, set aside.

Add a bit more oil to pan (if needed); heat; add green pepper, sauté until slightly soft; add onion slices, sauté until onion is translucent; add garlic; sauté for 1 minute more. Lower heat to low, return meat to pan, add tomatoes and water. Continue cooking for about 1 hour (or until meat is tender). If mixture appears too dry, add more water, a bit at a time to prevent meat from drying out.

Serving Ideas: Serve with mashed potatoes and fresh corn on the cob (or a green salad).

Prep Time: 15 minutes   Start to Finish: 1 hour 30 minutes   Servings: 4

Tray-Baked Pork Chops with Parsnips and Pears

Source: Len & Astrid Amico

Lucy's note: This dish is most delicious!

8 pork chops, thin cut

Marinade of rosemary, garlic and lemon, recipe below

3 parsnips

3 pears

Salt and pepper, to taste

MARINADE:

2 handfuls fresh rosemary, crushed

6 cloves garlic, very finely chopped

4 tablespoons olive oil

3 lemons, zested and juiced

Combine marinade ingredients in bowl. Rub and massage pork chops with marinade; place chops in large freezer bag with left over marinade. Place in refrigerator for 3 hours (or more).

About 1/2 hour before cooking pork chops preheat oven to 425 degrees.

While oven is heating up peel parsnips and pears. Core the pears; cut the pears and parsnips into 1/4 inch to 1/2 inch cubes. Place in roasting pan that has been sprayed with cooking spray; add pork chops and marinade. Toss together, lightly coat everything. Season with salt and pepper. Roast for 45 to 60 minutes, depending on the size of the pork chops.

Serving Ideas: Minty Bread Sauce is an optional accompaniment. The Bread Sauce packet can be found in an English food shop.

1 recipe Bread Sauce or packet

3 handfuls fresh mint, finely minced

2 teaspoons dry mustard

Combine all ingredients; spread over cooked pork chops, if desired.

Prep Time: 45 minutes   Start to Finish: 1 hour 30 minutes   Servings: 4

Veal Cutlets

Source: Lucy Peters

Vicki's note: Veal cutlets tend to be rather expensive, so this is always a treat when Mom makes them. This dish always reminds me of my brother Harry - I think it may be his all- time favorite meal!

2 pounds veal cutlets, sliced 1/4 inch thick

2 large eggs

1/4 cup milk

1 teaspoon salt

1/2 teaspoon pepper

2 cups Italian breadcrumbs

1/4 cup Romano or Parmesan cheese

1 1/2 teaspoons dried mint flakes

1/4 cup canola oil, or combination of olive oil and canola oil (for frying)

In a pie dish or shallow bowl beat eggs, milk, salt and pepper together. Set aside.

In a platter or other flat dish, mix bread crumbs, cheese and dried mint flakes. Stir well. Set aside.

Slightly pound cutlets with a meat mallet. You can also ask your butcher to do this at the grocery store. This helps to tenderize the meat. Don't pound too much or you will rip the meat. Dip each cutlet into egg mixture, then into breadcrumb mixture, pressing crumbs into each side gently. Place on a large dish. Continue until all cutlets are coated. Allow to sit for about 15 minutes before frying, to allow coating to adhere. It is a good idea to cover your dish with plastic wrap.

In the meantime, heat 1/8 cup oil over medium high heat in a large skillet. When you see "ripples" on top of oil, it is ready. Fry cutlets about 1 1/2 minutes per side. You'll cook in two batches. They cook very quickly, so watch carefully. Pan should be wiped out and fresh oil heated again, as described above, for each batch of cutlets,

Serving Ideas: The best sides to serve with these veal cutlets are mashed potatoes and stuffed artichokes and some crusty Italian bread. If you have any left over, these make wonderful cold meat sandwiches (on fresh Italian bread, of course).

This recipe can also be used with chicken cutlets and thin-cut pork chops. Reduce heat to medium. Cooking time will increase to 6 minutes per side for chicken and 3 minutes per side for pork chops

Prep Time: 15 minutes   Start to Finish: 20 minutes   Servings: 4

Veal Piccata

Source: Lucy Peters

Vicki's note: This is one of my favorite dishes that Mom makes!

1 1/2 pounds veal cutlets, 1/4" thick

1 large egg, beaten slightly with 2 tablespoons milk

1 cup all-purpose flour

1 teaspoon salt

1/2 teaspoon pepper

3 tablespoons olive oil, divided use

2 tablespoons butter, divided use

3/4 cup chicken stock, can use veal or beef stock

1/2 cup water

1/2 cup white wine, optional

4 teaspoons lemon juice, fresh is best

1/2 lemon, zested

1/4 cup capers, rinsed and drained

3 tablespoons Italian parsley, finely chopped, or 1 1/2 tablespoon dried

Slightly pound cutlets with a meat mallet. You can also ask your butcher to do this at the grocery store. This helps to tenderize the meat. Don't pound too much or you will rip the meat. Pat dry and set on plate.

Place egg and milk mixture in a container with sides (I use a shallow bowl). In similar dish mix flour, salt and pepper. Dip each slice of veal in the egg mixture, shake off excess, dip in flour mixture, coating both sides; shake off excess. Place in platter until all pieces are coated.

Heat 1 1/2 Tbsp. oil in a large skillet over medium heat. Melt 1/2 tablespoon of butter in skillet just before adding cutlets. Place veal in hot skillet, cooking 2 minutes per side. Remove from skillet, place on large platter and place in pre-heated oven, to keep warm. Repeat with remaining olive oil and 1/2 tbsp. butter to cook remaining cutlets.

Wipe out skillet, lower heat to medium low. Add stock water and wine (if using); bring to gentle boil. Continue boiling until sauce is reduced by half. Lower heat to low, add lemon juice, lemon zest, capers and remaining 1 tablespoon butter. Simmer for 5 minutes. Return veal cutlets to skillet, turning to coat both sides of cutlet. Place the cutlets in a serving platter, pour sauce over, sprinkle with chopped parsley.

Serving Ideas: This recipe can also be used with chicken cutlets. You would want to slice breasts to 1/4" thickness, and pound out as with the veal. Increase cooking time in skillet to 6 minutes per side as chicken takes a bit longer to cook.

Serving ideas: This dish is very good served with rice pilaf and Brussels sprouts or asparagus if it is in season.

Prep Time: 15 minutes   Start to Finish: 35 minutes   Servings: 4

The Amico Family – Lucy, Angelo, Sam, Joe, Lee, Rosie, Sally, Marianna, Leonard

1950's

Pastas

Vicki, Kelsey, and Uncle Joe
Stuffing Manicotti shells on Wednesday before Thanksgiving – the traditional
meal with sauce and meatballs on Wednesday night.
November 2007

Beef Risotto

Source: Sally Tudini

Vicki's note: This recipe is originally from Grandma Rosaria Vaccalluzzo, Lucy's grandmother.

1 tablespoon butter,
   or margarine

1 1/2 pounds lean ground beef

1 medium onion, chopped

1 clove garlic, minced

1 cup rice, uncooked

1 1/2 teaspoons salt

1 teaspoon dried basil

1 1/2 cups water

1 16 oz can crushed tomatoes

1 8 oz. can tomato sauce, or

1 cup homemade sauce

1/2 cup pimiento-stuffed
   green olives, sliced in half

1/3 cup Parmesan cheese, grated

Melt butter in a large pot over medium heat. Add beef, onion and garlic. Cook stirring often, until meat is slightly browned and onion is tender. Drain off excess water and/or fat. Stir in rice, salt, basil, water, tomatoes and tomato sauce.

Bring to a boil on medium high heat, then lower heat to simmer, cover pot and cook until rice is cooked (about 20 minutes for white rice; 40 minutes for brown rice). Fold in olives and half the cheese. Sprinkle with remaining cheese at serving time.

Fettuccini Alla Carbonara

Source: Joseph Amico

Vicki's note: This is a wonderful recipe from Uncle Joe

1/4 pound prosciutto
 ham, chopped fine
1 small onion, finely chopped
2 tablespoons olive oil
1 pound fettuccini
4 eggs, beaten
1/2 pint heavy whipping cream
 (bring to room temperature)
5 tablespoons fresh Italian
 parsley, chopped fine
 (2 tablespoons if dry)
1 teaspoon salt
1/2 teaspoon pepper
3/4 cup Romano cheese,
 separate use

Preheat oven to 250 degrees. Place an oven proof serving bowl, large enough to accommodate 1 pound fettuccini, in the oven. In a large pot add 1 Tbsp. of salt to 6 quarts of water and bring to a rapid boil.

While water is heating, chop prosciutto; set aside. Heat large skillet over medium heat, add 2 tablespoons olive oil, heat slightly, then add onion and sauté until translucent; add prosciutto; continue cooking for 2 more minutes. Remove from heat.

When water is at a rolling boil, add fettuccini and cook per package directions.

While fettuccini is cooking, beat together eggs and cream in a medium bowl. Stir in prosciutto, onions, 1/2 cup Romano cheese, parsley, salt and pepper. Set aside.

Remove bowl from oven. Drain fettuccini completely and place in pre-warmed bowl. Add liquid ingredients and toss quickly and thoroughly. Serve immediately with additional cheese.

Prep Time: 30 minutes

Servings: 4

Gnocchi

2 large potatoes (1 1/2 cups
  mashed), Instant potatoes
  may be used; see note below
1 tablespoon salt
2 tablespoons butter
2 1/2 cups flour

Peel and cut potatoes into 1 inch cubes. Boil potatoes in large pot of cold water with the 1 tablespoon of salt (cover to about 2 inches above potatoes). Cook until tender, about 20 to 30 minutes. (An under-cooked potato will ruin this dish!). Drain and mash potatoes with the butter (or use ricer). Allow to cool slightly. Add flour, 1/2 cup at a time. This may be done in an electric mixer with paddle beater. If mixing with a wooden spoon and dough becomes difficult to stir, place on a lightly floured surface and lightly knead by hand for a minute or two.

On a lightly floured surface, roll out dough into cigar- like ropes, about a foot long and no thicker than a finger. You will have several ropes. Cut into 1/2 inch slices. Roll each slice over fork prongs to form ridges (or use the small hole side of a grater), and poke finger lightly into one side to form a "belly button." Place prepared gnocchi on a floured towel, cover with another kitchen towel, and let dry for about two hours.

Bring a large pot of salted water to boil. Drop a few gnocchi into water to test. They will fall to bottom of pot, rising to the top when they are cooked. If they dissolve, it means they need more flour. If they rise to top, then you know they are fine. When gnocchi rise to the top allow them to cook for additional 20 to 30 seconds, then remove with slotted ladle to serving dish. Cook in batches, making sure not to overcrowd pot.

Top with sauce of your choice, i.e., any tomato sauce, butter-sage sauce, or pesto sauce. Sprinkle parmesan cheese over top.

Serving Ideas: If using instant mashed potatoes, cook as directed on box, using only the water called for. Follow directions for assembling gnocchi per directions above.

Prep Time: 50 minutes   Servings: 4

Lasagna

Source: Lucy Peters

Vicki's note: This is a Mom original. It doesn't get any better! In place of the ground beef you can substitute steamed vegetables for a vegetable lasagna that is equally as wonderful - see serving suggestions for ideas on this.

2 pounds ricotta cheese

3 medium eggs

3/4 cup mozzarella
   cheese, shredded

3/4 cup freshly grated Romano
   cheese (divided use)

1 tablespoon dried mint, or
   2 tablespoons fresh

1 pound lasagna noodles

1 pound extra lean ground beef

1/2 cup Italian flavored
   breadcrumbs

1 clove fresh garlic, minced

1/2 large onion, chopped

1 teaspoon dried basil, or
   2 teaspoons fresh

1 tablespoon parsley flakes
   or 2 tablespoons fresh

1/4 cup water

1 teaspoon salt

1/2 teaspoon pepper

4 cups tomato sauce

Pre-heat oven to 325 degrees.

In a large bowl combine ricotta, 2 of the eggs, mozzarella, 1/2 of the Romano cheese and the mint. Cover bowl and place in refrigerator for at least 45 minutes to give flavors a chance to blend (or prepare the day before - refrigerate until ready to use).

Bring large pot of water to boil - adding 1 tablespoon of salt and oil once the water begins to boil Cook lasagna noodles about 10 minutes - they should be tender but not soft. Drain in large colander and immediately run cold water over them to stop the cooking process and to cool enough to handle. Hang noodles over the side of the pot so they will not stick together and will be easy to handle when preparation begins.

WHILE NOODLES ARE COOKING: In a large bowl combine ground beef, bread crumbs, 1 egg, 1/4 cup Romano cheese, garlic, onion, basil, parsley, 1/4 cup water, salt and pepper. Sauté beef in large frying pan just until no longer pink; (do not to overcook). Remove from heat and drain if necessary. You don't want it to be greasy, so if it is too greasy, you can let it drain on paper towels on a plate.

In a 9" x 13" baking dish with enough sauce to cover bottom of pan, alternate layers of noodles, ricotta mixture, beef mixture, and sauce ending with noodles topped with sauce and sprinkled with Romano cheese. Bake in 325 degree oven for about 1 hour. If top begins to brown, cover with aluminum foil. Let stand covered about 10 minutes after removing from oven before cutting into squares. Serve with additional sauce and grated cheese.

Serving Ideas: FOR VEGETARIAN STYLE cook some broccoli flowerets, julienned carrots, julienned zucchini and chopped onion in a large frying pan until crisp tender - about 1/2 cup each. The broccoli and carrots can first be steamed briefly (about 3 minutes) in microwave in order to ensure even cooking of all vegetables. Use vegetables in place of the meat layer in lasagna.

Prep Time: 1 hour   Start to Finish: 1 hour 45 minutes   Servings: 10

Linguini with Eggplant and Tomatoes

Source: Vicki McNickle

Vicki's note: Mom and I got this recipe from the Chef at Saks Fifth Avenue Cafe in downtown San Francisco. It is wonderful! The sauce can be frozen or stored in refrigerator for a few weeks. Asia go cheese is used in this recipe because it's a lighter cheese than either Romano or Parmesan.

BASE SAUCE:

1 yellow onion, finely chopped

2 garlic cloves, whole

3/4 cup orange juice

1 28 oz. can chopped tomatoes

1/2 teaspoon salt

1/4 teaspoon pepper

1/2 tablespoon dry basil, or 1 1/2 tablespoons fresh – chopped

3/4 tablespoon balsamic vinegar

EGGPLANT PREP:

1 large eggplant, cut into 1" pieces

Olive oil cooking spray

1/2 teaspoon salt

1/4 teaspoon pepper

TOPPING:

2 large tomatoes, seeded and chopped into 1/2 inch cubes

Salt and pepper to taste

1/4 teaspoon garlic powder

1/4 teaspoon fresh basil, minced

1 pound linguini, or spaghetti

5 tablespoons grated Asagio cheese (or Romano)

Sauté onion with garlic (leave cloves whole to poach) for 5 to 10 minutes in large sauce pan until onions are translucent. Add orange juice and let cook down on low - medium heat for about 5 to 10 minutes. Add tomatoes, salt, pepper and basil (if using dried basil) and continue cooking for 35 to 45 minutes on low - medium heat. In the last 5 minutes of cooking add basil (if using fresh) and vinegar. Once tomatoes have been added to sauce start your pasta water to boil.

While sauce is cooking, cube eggplant into bite-sized pieces. Spray with olive oil cooking spray; Toss with salt and pepper. Roast in glass baking dish for about 20 to 25 minutes in 400 degree oven.

As sauce and eggplant are cooking, cube plum tomatoes and mix in bowl with salt, pepper, garlic powder, and basil (minced). Set aside.

During last ten minutes of cooking sauce and eggplant, add pasta to boiling water. Cook for 7 minutes or until al dente. When sauce is cooked, remove from heat and puree in blender until smooth. Place 1/4 to 1/2 cup sauce on plate, sprinkle with 1 Tbsp. grated Asia go cheese. Place 1 cup pasta over cheese, sprinkle with some of the eggplant and tomatoes. Sprinkle additional cheese on top if desired.

Prep Time: 15 minutes   Start to Finish: 1 hour   Servings: 5

Manicotti

Source: Lucy Peters

Vicki's note: Thanksgiving would not be complete without manicotti. It has been a tradition for many years now to eat them on Wednesday night for dinner. In the old, old days, we would have manicotti as our first course for Thanksgiving dinner, then we would wash all the dishes, and have a full traditional Thanksgiving dinner. Several years ago we figured out that it was just too much in one day! We then shifted the tradition. Mom's homemade meatballs and sauce with manicotti are a taste that is just out of this world! This recipe is from Aunt Gina and originally from her mother Mae Syracuse.

MANICOTTI SHELLS:

2 cups water

2 cups flour

4 eggs, slightly beaten

1/2 teaspoon salt

MANICOTTI FILLING:

2 pounds ricotta cheese

1/2 lb. mozzarella cheese

1/4 cup Pecorino Romano cheese

2 eggs, beaten (If eggs
    are small use 3)

2 1/2 teaspoons dried mind flakes

3/4 teaspoon salt

1/4 teaspoon pepper

10 cups spaghetti sauce,
    see recipe in book

5 tablespoons Pecorino Romano
    cheese (for sprinkling on top)

SHELLS

Beat flour and water first, then beat in egg and salt. Cover and let stand 1 hour at room temperature. If the batter seems thick before you start or as you are making them, add a little more water to thin batter out. Crepes should be light and thin, NOT thick and heavy. Stack on wax paper-lined plate. Make shells ahead of time and cool. These can be stored in freezer for a few months in airtight container or bag.

IF you do not have a crepe pan follow these instructions to make in a frying pan: Lightly oil a frying pan and then heat the pan for about a minute over medium high heat. Spoon approximately two or three tablespoons of batter into the middle of the hot frying pan. Quickly and carefully tilt the pan in a circular motion until the batter forms a round, thin layer in the pan. (Similar to a crepe or a very thin pancake.) Cook about 1 or 2 minutes until the shell surface appears dry. Carefully turn the manicotti shell over using a spatula, and cook for an additional 30 seconds. If you have a crepe' maker, follow directions for making crepe's per instructions provided.

FILLING / ASSEMBLY

In a large bowl mix cheeses, eggs, mint, salt and pepper. Cover bowl and put into fridge for 1 hour (or up to 8 hours) to let flavors meld.

Preheat oven to 325 degrees. Put thin layer of sauce on bottom of cookie sheet - enough to cover bottom. To assemble manicotti: Fill each manicotti shell by placing one heaping teaspoon of filling into center of each shell spread down middle, but leave a little space at edge. Roll up and place seam side down on baking pan which has been lined with sauce. Place next to one another, but DO NOT overcrowd pan or layer. Once pan is filled, spoon thin layer of sauce over top of shells. Sprinkle with Romano cheese. Bake in 325 degree oven for 30 to 40 minutes. Remove from oven and cover with aluminum foil. Let stand for about 5 to 10 minutes before serving - this lets the cheese firm up so they won't be runny. Serve with extra sauce and cheese on the side.

Serving Ideas: Use shallow pans, such as bottom of broiler pan. Do not stack manicotti. Stuffed shells may be made ahead and frozen (in single layers). They don't have to be defrosted before placing in oven. Just add 10-15 min. to cooking time.

Prep Time: 1 hour 30 minutes   Start to Finish: 2 hours   Servings: 40

Pasta (homemade)

Source: Lucy Peters

Lucy's note: I don't remember who gave me this recipe; but I do remember Grandma making pasta with these same ingredients. It was always a treat to have her hand made pasta.

4 cups flour

1 teaspoon salt

5 medium eggs

1 tablespoon olive oil

8 tablespoons cold water,
**   more if needed**

Place flour and salt in bowl of food processor fitted with pastry blade. In a separate small bowl, lightly beat eggs. Stir oil into eggs to combine. Add egg mixture to the food processor, using "pulse" to combine ingredients, scraping down sides once or twice. With machine running, add cold water a little at a time until dough is desired consistency - about 1 minute. The dough should stick together if pinched between fingers and be cornmeal yellow in color. If needed, more flour may be added, A LITTLE AT A TIME.

Let dough "rest" for about 1/2 hour. Roll dough (small sections at a time) on floured surface into sheets about 8 inches wide; 12 inches long; and 1/16 inch thick. Fold over several times. Cut into desired thickness. Unfold noodles onto floured surface and let stand to dry - about 30 minutes. Cook pasta in rapidly boiling water for only 2 to 3 min. Fresh pasta cooks very rapidly.

NOTE: If you have a pasta machine, you can use that instead of rolling out pasta by hand, however, you will still just do a bit at a time.

Pasta Con Broccoli

Source: Lucy Peters

Vicki's note: Grandma Amico made this on Friday nights because when you're a good Catholic, you don't eat meat on Fridays. As with many of the great Italian recipes I have, Grandma passed it along to Mom who then passed it along to me.

If you don't like anchovies and are thinking of omitting them, I would encourage you to try it this way at least once this way. It really doesn't taste fishy - the anchovies give this dish a nice nutty and salty taste that is DELICIOUS!

1 16 oz. can chicken broth

1 pound linguini

1 pound broccoli, large bunch

2 tablespoons olive oil

2 large garlic cloves, chopped very fine

1 2 oz. can boneless anchovies, drained (optional) (see serving ideas)

1/4 teaspoon crushed red pepper flakes (optional) this will give it a little "kick"

1 teaspoon salt, if not using anchovies

1/4 teaspoon black pepper, 1/2 teaspoon if not using crushed red pepper

1 teaspoon dried parsley

4 tablespoons Romano cheese, for sprinkling on top

In large pot bring 2 quarts of water along with chicken broth and salt to a boil.

While the water is coming to a boil, wash and cut up broccoli (both flowerets and stems) into bite size pieces. When cutting the stems, it is a good idea to remove the bottom inch, and then peel the outer part of the stems to get off the rough outer layer. Add broccoli pieces to boiling water and cook for about 5-7 minutes. Broccoli should be "crispy tender". Remove with slotted spoon when the broccoli is cooked and transfer to a large bowl. You will cook the pasta in the boiling water next, so don't throw that away! Let water come back to a boil and add pasta - cook according to package instructions.

While the pasta is cooking, heat olive oil in large frying pan over low heat. Cook garlic for about 1 minute then add anchovies (if using) - they will actually 'melt' in the pan - stir constantly with wooden spoon, pressing down to break them apart. There will still be some small pieces left. Once this has occurred, then add a cup of the pasta water, crushed red pepper (optional), parsley and broccoli back to pan. Sauté at medium low. Heat stirring continuously but gently so you don't break up the broccoli. Continue sautéing until pasta is cooked.

Remove and reserve 1/2 cup of cooking liquid from pasta pot. Drain pasta, put into large serving bowl and stir in broccoli/garlic mixture. More liquid may be added to individual bowls, if desired (from liquid reserved). Serve with Romano cheese.

Serving Ideas: If anchovies are not boneless, you will want to remove the bone before using by gently spreading apart and removing the strip of small bones in the middle.

Prep Time: 10 minutes   Start to Finish: 30 minutes   Servings: 4

Pasta Giuseppe

Source: Joseph Amico

Vicki's note: This is an original of Uncle Joe's. He adapted it from several different dishes he'd eaten or recipes read.

3/4 package frozen artichoke
hearts, thawed, drained
and cut in quarters

1 pound chicken breast,
boneless, skinless

3 tablespoons olive oil,
separate use

1 small onion, thinly sliced

1 cup mushroom, sliced

3/4 cup kalamata olives,
pitted and sliced in half

2 cloves garlic, finely minced

2 large tomatoes, large, seeded
and cut into 1" chunks (see
serving suggestions also)

2 tablespoons fresh parsley,
finely chopped or 1
tablespoon dried

2 tablespoons fresh basil
leaves, cut into strips
or 1 tablespoon dried

3/4 cup chicken broth

1/2 cup white wine

1 pound linguini, or
thin spaghetti

5 tablespoons Romano cheese

Remove artichoke hearts from freezer and allow to sit at room temperature to thaw. Put in single layer on paper towels to absorb excess moisture.

Rinse chicken breasts and pat dry with paper towels. Pound chicken breasts with mallet or bottom of flat heavy cup. It's a good idea to do this on a cutting board between sheets of wax paper. Pound just enough to thin it out, but not so much that you cause holes. Cut breasts into 2 inch strips. Heat 2 tablespoons olive oil over medium heat in a large sauté pan. Sauté chicken strips very quickly in very hot oil olive oil, stirring constantly. Remove from pan. Set aside. You may have to do this in batches - don't overcrowd the pan or the chicken will steam and you want to fry it so it is slightly browned.

Once chicken is cooked put a large pot of water on to boil for the pasta. Add to the water 1 tablespoon of salt.

Wipe out pan if there are a lot of chicken pieces stuck to bottom. In same pan heat one tablespoon oil over low heat. Add onion and sauté until translucent, 8 to 10 minutes. Add sliced mushrooms; sauté until slightly softened, 5 to 6 minutes. Add artichoke hearts, olives and garlic - heat through about 5 minutes. Add tomatoes, parsley and basil, and simmer for 3 to 4 minutes. Add chicken broth, wine and chicken strips - stir gently. Continue simmering (stirring once or twice) for 10 minutes. Remove from heat.

In last ten minutes of cooking sauce, add pasta to boiling water and cook per package directions.

Once pasta is cooked, drain, reserving 2 cups of the cooking water. Return pasta to empty pot, add sauce, stirring carefully. Reserved water may be added at this time, if more moisture is desired. Serve pasta with cheese on the side.

Serving Ideas: If you don't like the skin on the tomatoes, you can immerse in pasta water once it is boiling and before the pasta is added, for about 30 seconds. Remove with slotted spoon and let cool enough to handle. Skin will gently peel away. Cut tomatoes in half seed and cut into 1 inch chunks.

Pasta Primavera

Source: Joseph Amico

Vicki's note: I can remember going to Uncle Joe's house for dinner in Buffalo. In those days I smoked, and in the thick of winter, with the wind blowing and snow storming, we would have to go outside to smoke. In those days I just thought he was being anal (which he probably was), but now I have a greater appreciation for his point of view. Besides that, it would have ruined the aroma of his wonderful cooking that we so enjoyed. I miss those days. I have very fond memories of my Uncle Joe and a lot of wonderful time spent with him.

4 tablespoons olive
   oil, divided use

1 small onion, finely chopped

2 garlic cloves, minced

1 cup Italian eggplant, peeled
   and cubed into 1" pieces

3/4 cup white mushrooms, sliced

2 15 oz. cans chicken broth

1/2 cup white wine, dry

1/2 cup carrot, julienned
   into 1 1/2" strips

1/2 cup cauliflower flowerets

1/2 cup broccoli flowerets

1 pound spaghetti, or farfalle
   pasta (bow ties)

2 medium tomatoes,
   chopped coarsely

1/2 cup snow peas, sliced

1 pinch dill

1 pinch thyme

2 tablespoons fresh parsley,
   minced (or 1 Tbsp. dry)

1 1/2 teaspoons salt

1 teaspoon pepper

4 tablespoons Romano cheese

Put large pot of water onto boil to which you have added 1 tablespoon salt.

In a deep 12" skillet heat 2 tablespoons olive oil over medium heat. Add onion and cook for 3 minutes. Add 2 more tablespoons olive oil and heat one minute. Add eggplant and mushrooms, cook for 3 minutes. Lower heat to low and add garlic. Cook for 1 minute more, stirring as to not burn garlic. Add chicken broth and wine and remove from heat.

Clean and cut carrots, cauliflower and broccoli. Place cut vegetables into the large pot of boiling pasta water prior to adding pasta. Let cook for 4 minutes. Using slotted spoon remove from water and add to pan with other vegetables, broth and wine.

Let water come back to a boil. Once water is boiling, add pasta and cook per package instructions

While pasta is cooking return vegetables to a medium heat, add tomatoes, peas, herbs, spices and salt and pepper to taste. Bring veggies to a boil. Immediately lower heat and simmer until pasta is done. Place pasta in dishes, ladle veggies over pasta. Top with plenty of Romano cheese.

Pasta with Eggs & Butter

Source: Lucy Peters

Vicki's note: This recipe is from Mom. Next to manicotti, this was my favorite way to eat pasta when I was a kid. The butter, eggs and cheese were soothing foods to me. Mom often made this on Friday nights as I recall as our "no meat" meal.

1 pound spaghetti, or linguini

6 eggs

8 tablespoons butter

1 teaspoon salt

1/2 teaspoon pepper

1 teaspoon garlic powder

4 tablespoons Romano cheese

Bring large pot of water to boil to which 1 Tbsp. salt has been added. Cook pasta per package directions. Remove from heat. DO NOT DRAIN. Remove about 2 cups of the cooking water into a large measuring cup or small pan, leaving about 2 cups of cooking water in pot with pasta.

While pasta is cooking, beat eggs in medium bowl with salt, pepper, butter and garlic powder. Set aside until pasta is cooked.

Return pot to stove (over low heat). When water with pasta begins to boil, add egg mixture in a slow steady stream, stirring continuously. Cook until eggs are firm and butter has melted. If mixture gets too thick, add some of the reserved liquid.

Serve in pasta bowls with Romano cheese sprinkled on top.

Prep Time: 5 minutes   Start to Finish: 20 minutes   Servings: 4

Pasta with Fried Zucchini

Source: Lucy Peters

Lucy's note: Necessity is the mother of invention" it is said. I believed Grandma Amico had "invented" this dish as an economical way to feed her large family. Imagine my surprise and delight when I saw this recipe in a "Bon Appetit" magazine!!

2 tablespoons olive oil

1 pound small zucchini,
   sliced 1/4" thick

1/2 teaspoon salt

1/4 teaspoon pepper

1 pound thin spaghetti

2 teaspoons salt

1/4 cup fresh basil, cut into strips

1/4 cup Romano cheese, grated

Bring large pot of water to boil, with 1 tablespoon salt.

While water is coming to a boil, heat olive oil in medium sized frying pan. Add the zucchini slices sprinkled with salt and pepper to taste. Sauté over medium-low heat until zucchini slices are light brown on both sides - about 10 minutes. Remove from oil and drain on paper towels. Place in a small bowl and set aside.

Cook spaghetti per package directions. Before draining pasta, take 1 cup of the pasta cooking water and add to zucchini. Drain the spaghetti and transfer to a large serving bowl. Add half the zucchini slices, basil and Romano cheese - toss gently. Place remaining zucchini slices on top of pasta in bowl and serve.

Serving Ideas: NOTE: This same recipe may be made with eggplant. Substitute with eggplant that has been sliced about the same thickness and then cut in quarters. Proceed as above

Pasta with Peas

Source: Lucy Peters

Lucy's note: When fresh peas were in season Grandma Amico liked to make this pasta dish using the freshly shucked peas and her own home bottled tomatoes.

1 tablespoon olive oil

1 small yellow onion,
   chopped fine

1 clove garlic, finely minced

1 28 oz. can crushed tomatoes

1 cup water

1 tablespoon dried basil

1/2 teaspoon salt

1/4 teaspoon pepper

1 14.5 oz. can low sodium
   chicken broth

1 10 oz. package frozen peas

1 pound ditalini, or
   other small pasta

Romano cheese

Heat olive oil on medium high heat in medium sauce pan. Sauté onion until translucent, 8 to 10 minutes... Add garlic, sauté for 1 minute. Add tomatoes, water, basil, salt and pepper and chicken broth. Bring to boil, reduce heat and simmer sauce for 40 minutes. Remove from heat, stir in peas.

In last 20 minutes of cooking sauce, bring large pot of water to boil with 1 tablespoon salt.

Cook pasta per package directions. Drain, reserving 2 cups of the cooking water. Stir sauce into drained pasta in large serving bowl. Add some of the reserved water, if more liquid is desired. Sprinkle cheese over top when serving.

Serving Ideas: For asparagus lovers: substitute 1 lb. fresh or 10oz. package asparagus for peas. If using frozen, proceed as for the frozen peas. If using fresh, cut asparagus into 1 inch pieces and cook until tender.

Prep Time: 15 minutes   Start to Finish: 1 hour   Servings: 4

Pasta with Stewed Tomatoes & Spinach

Source: Vicki McNickle

Vicki's note: In the old days, they would make up different ways to cook pasta for economical reasons. I made up this dish as a way to put something together quickly and easily using what I already had on hand. Maybe it's a sign of the times!

1 pound pasta, shells or elbows

1 package frozen spinach, or
** 1 pound. fresh - see serving ideas**

2 16 oz. cans stewed tomatoes

1/2 teaspoon garlic powder

1 teaspoon salt and pepper

2 tablespoons Romano
** cheese, grated**

Bring large pot of water to boil to which 1 tablespoon salt has been added. Cook pasta per package directions.

While pasta is cooking, cook spinach per package directions. Once cooked, press spinach into colander to get all the water to drain out if using fresh spinach, see "serving ideas" for alternate preparation.

In a medium bowl, mash stewed tomatoes. Set aside. When pasta is cooked, drain and return to pot. Add tomatoes, spinach, garlic powder, salt and pepper and mix well. If using Italian sausage (see serving ideas), add that now as well. Warm up pasta with spinach and tomatoes for about 5 minutes in pot. Serve hot with grated cheese on top.

Serving Ideas: If using fresh spinach, you can cook it in a large pot to which one tablespoon olive oil has been heated. Clean spinach and added to heated oil with excess water still clinging onto leaves. Cook covered for three minutes. Turn off heat, and let spinach sit in pan until ready to mix with pasta. Use spinach water when adding to pasta as it will add to the flavors. Adding cooked Italian sausage to the dish is a tasty variation. Slice up two links into 1 inch slices; sauté in pan until cooked. Hot Italian bread and a salad are a good accompaniment to this fast and easy dish.

Prep Time: 15 minutes   Start to Finish: 30 minutes   Servings: 4

Spinach Ravioli with Sage Butter Sauce

Source: Vicki McNickle

Vicki's note: This recipe was created while testing the homemade pasta recipe in the book - my family loves it!

NOTE: Frozen spinach can be used instead of freshly made, however, in both cases make sure to drain spinach in a colander and press against sides to remove all excess moisture. Too much moisture in the spinach will make the filling watery and cause the ravioli to fall apart.

homemade pasta dough (see recipe in book)

1 pound whole milk ricotta cheese

1 large egg

4 ounces mozzarella cheese, shredded

1/2 teaspoon salt

1/4 teaspoon pepper

1 teaspoon dried mint flakes

1 pound chopped spinach, cooked, cooled and drained

1/2 cup shredded Parmesan cheese, divided use

1 egg white

8 tablespoons butter

16 fresh sage leaves

1 large lemon, juiced

SHELLS, FILLING AND ASSEMBLY:

Make pasta per recipe in book. While pasta dough is "resting" mix the ricotta cheese, egg, mozzarella, salt, pepper, mint, drained spinach (see note above) and 1/4 cup parmesan cheese in large bowl. Make sure to mix well, fully incorporating the egg. Cover and put in fridge to let the flavors meld until ready to fill ravioli shells. Take out about 5 minutes before filling.

Roll out pasta dough on large cutting board (you will have to do in batches) to 1/8 inch thickness. Cut into "rounds" about 2 inches in diameter. You can use a small glass or cookie cutter if you don't have a ravioli cutter. As you cut rounds, place them on a cookie sheet that has been lined with parchment paper, and lightly dusted with flour. Do not stack rounds: put a piece of parchment paper between layers. Once all rounds are cut, you are ready to fill. Beat one egg white (discard yolk) in a small bowl. You will use this to "seal" the edges of ravioli.

If you are going to cook now, put a large pot with 6 to 8 quarts of salted water on to boil while you are filling the ravioli. It should be rapidly boiling before cooking ravioli.

Take about 1 teaspoon of filling and put in middle of round. Dip your finger into the egg white, and then spread on outer edge of round. Immediately place another round on top and 'pinch' edges together to seal. NOTE: You want to make sure to not overfill ravioli so filling will not push out. As ravioli are made, return to parchment-lined cookie sheet. Do not stack on top of one another except if you have a sheet of parchment between layers. Once all ravioli are filled, cook, or store in fridge for up to one day. Make sure they are covered with plastic warp if you're not going to cook right away.

SAUCE:

While pasta water is coming to a boil and before cooking ravioli, make sage sauce. Melt butter in 12 to 14 inch sauté pan and continue cooking until golden brown color appears in the thinnest liquid of the butter. Add sage leaves and remove from heat. Add lemon juice and set aside.

FINISHED PRODUCT:

To cook ravioli, gently drop about 8 into rapidly boiling water - they will sink to the bottom. Once they float to the top, they will be done. Remove from water with a slotted spoon and place into serving bowl; repeat until all ravioli are cooked. As you move cooked ravioli to serving bowl, add small amounts of sauce to pan to prevent ravioli from sticking. Cover dish to keep warm. Cook in batches – you don't want to overcrowd pan or ravioli will stick together.

Serving Ideas: This butter sage sauce can also be used on other pasta recipes.

Prep Time: 2 hours   Start to Finish: 2 Hrs. 25 minutes   Servings: 6

Lucy and Marshall Peters

1980's

Rosie Giambroni, Marianna Amico, Lucy Peters
Lucy was in her 20's in this photo, not sure about Aunt Rosie and Grandma.
This was taken out in front of Grandma and Grandpa's house on Busty.

Coconut Meringue Pie

Source: Peg Miller

Vicki's notes: This is a rich but wonderful pie.

- 1 frozen pie shell, 9" baked per package instructions
- 2 cups milk
- 1/4 teaspoon salt
- 1/2 cup sugar
- 1 cup shredded coconut
- 3 tablespoons cornstarch
- 3 tablespoons water
- 4 egg yolks, reserve whites for later use
- 1 tablespoon butter, room temperature
- 1 teaspoon vanilla
- 6 egg whites
- 1/4 teaspoon cream of tartar
- 6 tablespoons sugar
- 1/4 cup shredded coconut

Follow package directions for baking pie shell. Once pie shell is cooked, preheat oven to 400 degrees.

FILLING:

In a medium sauce pan combine milk, sugar, salt and coconut. Cook over medium heat until mixture is very hot, but DO NOT ALLOW TO BOIL. In a small bowl, mix cornstarch with 3 tbsp. water. In a medium bowl, beat egg yolks, then blend in cornstarch and water mixture. Add about 1/4 cup of the warm milk mixture to the egg mixture and then add it all to the milk mixture in the pan. Cook and stir about 2 to 3 minutes over medium heat. Remove from heat. Add butter and vanilla, stir to combine - butter should be melted into liquid. Cool mixture, then pour into 9 inch baked and cooled pie shell. Set aside.

MERINGUE:

Beat egg whites with cream of tartar on medium speed until soft peaks form. Continue beating while adding sugar, 1 tbsp. at a time. Beat on high until stiff glossy peaks form and sugar is dissolved. Spread evenly over filling, sealing edges to crust. Sprinkle with shredded coconut.

Bake at 400 degrees until meringue is lightly browned, 5 to 10 minutes Cool completely before cutting.

Custard Pie

Source: Sally Tudini

9" unbaked pie shell, thawed

1 egg white

3 eggs, beaten

1 1/2 cups milk

1/2 cup sugar

1/4 teaspoon salt

1 teaspoon vanilla

1 tablespoon butter, melted

1/4 teaspoon cinnamon

Pinch nutmeg

Preheat oven to 450 degrees.

Beat egg white in a small bowl; with a pastry brush, brush egg white on bottom and sides of unbaked pie crust (that has been thawed); set aside.

Mix remaining ingredients in medium bowl and pour into prepared pie shell. Place pie on a cookie sheet (to catch any boil over). Place on lower rack of oven. Bake for 15 minutes at 450 degrees. Reduce oven temperature to 325 degrees. Continue baking for 30 minutes or until knife inserted into center comes out clean.

Prep Time: 30 minutes   Start to Finish: 1 hour   Servings: 8

Lemon Meringue Pie

Source: Lucy Peters

Lucy's note: This was my sister Rosie's specialty. She made the BEST lemon pie. She made it often for Grandma and Grandpa. It was the only pie that they truly enjoyed!

1 pie shell, 9" baked

1/4 cup flour

5 tablespoons cornstarch

1 teaspoon Salt

1 1/2 cups sugar

2 1/4 cups boiling water

3 egg yolks (reserve whites for meringue)

1/2 cup lemon juice, plus 1 tablespoon zest

1 teaspoon butter

1/4 teaspoon cream of tartar

3 tablespoons sugar

Bake pie shell according to package directions.

For pie, preheat oven to 400 degrees once shell is cooked and out of oven.

FILLING:

Mix flour, cornstarch, salt, sugar and boiling water. Cook in top of double boiler over simmering water or over direct low heat about 15 minutes, or until thickened and clear, stirring constantly. Add lightly beaten egg yolks and cook 2 minutes longer. Add lemon juice, zest and butter; stir to combine. Remove from heat. Cool slightly, then turn into baked pie shell.

MERINGUE:

Beat egg whites with cream of tartar until frothy. Add sugar 1 tbsp. at a time. Continue beating until eggs whites are stiff but not dry. Spoon meringue over pie, completely covering filling. Place pie in oven to brown slightly, about 5 to 10 minutes.

Prep Time: 15 minutes   Start to Finish: 1 hour   Servings: 8

Pumpkin Ice Cream Pie

Source: Lucy Peters

Vicki's note: This recipe is from a restaurant in Buffalo, NY. Next to pumpkin Gelato, I don't think desert gets any better than this!

1 9" pie shell, baked

1 quart vanilla ice
  cream, softened

1 cup canned pumpkin

1/2 cup sugar

1/4 teaspoon salt

1/4 teaspoon ginger

1/4 teaspoon nutmeg

1/4 teaspoon cinnamon

2 cups heavy cream or whipping
  cream, divided use

SYRUP: (optional)

1/4 cup hot water

1/2 cup brown sugar

1/4 cup dark corn syrup

1/2 teaspoon vanilla

Bake pie shell according to package instructions. Cool completely before proceeding.

FILLING

Spread softened ice cream in cooled pie shell. Place in freezer until thoroughly hardened (cover with plastic wrap). Blend together pumpkin, sugar, salt and spices. In a separate bowl, whip 1 cup of heavy cream until stiff peaks form; fold into pumpkin mixture. Spoon over frozen ice cream. Place in freezer (covered with plastic wrap) for at least 2 hours, or until ready to serve.

Just before serving, whip second cup of heavy cream with 1 tbsp. sugar until stiff peaks form. Frost pie with whipped cream, drizzle with syrup if desired (recipe follows) and serve.

SYRUP

In a small pot, bring water, sugar and corn syrup to a boil. Continue to boil until the mixture starts to thicken. Remove from heat. When syrup is cool, stir in vanilla and drizzle over pie.

Serving Ideas: 3/4 tsp. pumpkin pie spice may be substituted for the three spices.

Prep Time: 45 minutes   Start to Finish: 3 hours   Servings: 8

Pumpkin Torte

Source: Alice Peters

Lucy's note: From Alice Peters who is Marshall's brother Carl's wife. She's a great cook and makes the best desserts! Alice and Carl live in Shawana, Wisconsin.

CRUST

1 1/2 cups graham cracker crumbs

1/2 cup butter, melted

1/4 cup chopped walnuts,
  lightly toasted

FIRST LAYER

8 ounces cream cheese, softened

2 eggs, beaten

1/2 cup sugar

TOP LAYER

1 envelope gelatin powder,
  unflavored

1 1/2 cups canned pumpkin

3 egg yolks, slightly beaten

1/2 cup milk

1/2 cup sugar

1/2 teaspoon salt

1 teaspoon pumpkin pie spice

1/4 cup cold water

3 egg whites

1 tablespoon sugar

whipped cream, optional

Heat oven to 350 degrees. Prepare 9" x 13" torte or pie pan by spraying with cooking spray. Set aside.

CRUST:

Mix together graham cracker crumbs, melted butter and chopped nuts. Press into prepared pan. Set aside.

FIRST LAYER:

Beat together softened cream cheese and sugar until well mixed. Add beaten eggs and mix thoroughly. Pour into prepared crust and bake for 20 minutes.

TOP LAYER:

Dissolve packet of gelatin in 1/4 cup cold water. Set aside.

In a medium saucepan, mix together next six ingredients (pumpkin to pumpkin pie spice). Cook over medium heat, stirring constantly, until thickened (this mixture will not be as thick as a pudding). Remove from heat, stir in dissolved gelatin. Set aside to cool thoroughly.

Beat egg whites with 1 Tbsp sugar until soft peaks form. Fold gently into cooled pumpkin mixture. Pour over baked cream cheese layer. Cover with plastic wrap and chill in refrigerator until firm (about 45 minutes).

Serving Ideas: If desired, Torte may be topped with whipped cream when served.

Prep Time: 45 minutes   Start to Finish: 1 hour 50 minutes   Servings: 12

Taylor, Stan, Jason, Leah and Grandma Lucy

Summer, 2001

Pizza

Source: Sandy Amico

Vicki's note: When we were kids a holiday was not complete without Aunt Sandy's pizza! We've missed her these past few years on Thanksgiving, and her pizza. These days Kelsey asks me to make homemade pizza on special occasions. I love that she likes this - it's like sharing one of my childhood favorite traditions with her!

1 package hot roll mix

1 package active dry yeast (if not included in box of roll mix)

2 tablespoons olive oil (for pizza pan)

2 1/2 cups pizza sauce (see recipe in book)

2 tablespoons Pecorino Romano cheese

OPTIONS FOR TOPPINGS:

1 stick pepperoni, sliced thin

8 medium mushrooms, sliced thin

1 cup olives (green and/or black), sliced in half

1 cup artichoke hearts, sliced in quarters - completely dried

1/4 pound salami, sliced thin

1/2 pound Italian sausage, sliced thin (or crumbled) and cooked

1 bell pepper, sliced thin

1/2 medium Bermuda onion, sliced thin

2 cups mozzarella cheese, grated

If not already made, prepare your pizza sauce first, then while it's cooking, proceed with making your pizza dough and cutting up toppings. See recipe in book for sauce.

Pizza Dough: Most boxes of roll mix come with instructions and yeast. However, check your package when purchased to insure it includes yeast. Follow the instructions on the box for the dough. This will include steps such as: Mix well and form into ball. Roll in enough flour to prevent sticking. Place ball into lightly greased bowl, cover with dish towel, set in warm place, and allow to rise until doubled in size; punch down; knead a few minutes and let rise again.

When dough is about half way finished, preheat oven to 450 degrees. Slice toppings - trying to make them of similar sizes so they cook evenly. If using sausage, cook in a separate pan before using as a topping.

When dough is ready punch down a bit. On a floured surface, roll out pizza to the size you want. Dust your hands with flour to keep the dough from sticking. Gently stretch the dough using the back of your floured hands, letting the weight of the dough pull the dough thinner. Use the backs of your fingers to push the dough out wider. Start in the middle of the dough with both hands close together, and slowly pull your hands apart, allowing the dough to glide above your hands. Turn the dough about 15 degrees on your hands and repeat this step until the dough is thinner, wider, and consistent throughout the entire circumference of the crust.

Sprinkle cornmeal on a medium cookie sheet or pizza stone and place dough you just shaped in pan. If you like a thinner crust, you will most likely get two 12 inch pizzas from this. If you like a thicker crust, you may only get one. If this is your preference, then you can cut above amounts in half. I prefer thinner - this is a more "traditional" Italian style pizza (see serving note under serving ideas). Using a fork, prick middle of pizza several times so that air bubbles will not form during cooking. Cover with 1 to 1 1/4 cup tomato sauce.

Sprinkle with 1 Tbsp Romano cheese. Add desired toppings (see note under 'serving ideas).

Place in 450 degree preheated oven on bottom rack of oven. Bake for about 12 to 15 minutes until bottom is lightly browned. If cooking two pizza's switch racks half way through cooking. Bottom of pizza crust should be lightly browned and crispy - if it isn't you may need to leave it in longer. I suggest making only one pizza in the oven at a time - they cook faster and more evenly.

Remove from oven and spread with 1 cup grated mozzarella cheese (on each). Return to oven and cook until cheese is melted, about 5 minutes. If you'd like you can add the cheese under the toppings - then just eliminate this step.

Serving Ideas: If you don't have pizza pans or a pizza stone, you can purchase disposable ones from the grocery store and they work very well. I suggest you punch a few holes in the bottom first with a sharp knife (carefully) before putting in crust.

When we were in Italy a few years back, we were surprised to find that pizza there comes with a very thin crust, and has very little sauce and toppings. I have found that this is a much more enjoyable way to be able to "taste" all the ingredients and really enjoy your pizza! If you have not had it this way, I encourage you to give it a try!

Final note: while making pizza may seem like a daunting task, it is actually quite easy and can be a lot of fun to have family and friends join in on the process. My kids love this pizza!

You can "cheat" by using a Boboli from the grocery store instead of homemade crust for this - while not as good, still fun! Instead of using pizza pans, you can use a cookie sheet.

Prep Time: 1 hour   Start to Finish: 1 hour 25 minutes   Servings: 8

Pizza Sauce

Source: Lucy Peters

Lucy's note: This is Grandma Amico's recipe. There is no comparison between this sauce and kind you get from a jar or even your local restaurant. The little extra time is well worth the effort.

Vicki's note: I like to puree my sauce before using on pizza, but this is not necessary if you like a chunkier sauce. If you don't have time to make a homemade crust you can use a Boboli instead and you have great pizza in no time!

1 tablespoon olive oil

1/2 medium onion, chopped fine

1 clove garlic, minced

1 28 oz. can crushed
   tomatoes, in puree

1 1/2 teaspoons dried basil

1 teaspoon oregano

1 teaspoon sugar

1 tablespoon butter

1/2 teaspoon salt

1/4 teaspoon pepper

Heat oil on medium heat, add onion and cook until translucent, 6-8 minutes. Add garlic and cook one more minute.

While onions are cooking puree tomatoes in blender.

Add remaining ingredients, bring to boil, then lower heat and simmer. Cook for 45 minutes stirring often.

Sauce is enough for 3 12 inch pizzas or 2 if you like a lot of sauce.

Poultry

Sally Tudini, Sam Amico, Lucy Peters

They were all so young! Of Mom's siblings, Aunt Sally was the oldest, Uncle Sam was just a few years younger than her and Mom was the youngest of the seven children.

Baked Chicken

Source: Lucy Peters

2 tablespoons olive oil

1/4 cup lemon juice

4 chicken breasts, skinless
   and boneless

2 cups cornflake crumbs

1 teaspoon paprika

1 teaspoon dried parsley

1/4 teaspoon dried mint
   flakes (optional)

1/4 teaspoon salt

1/4 teaspoon black pepper

2 teaspoons olive oil
   (this is additional)

Preheat oven to 400 degrees. Coat 9" x 13" baking dish with cooking spray, or lightly oil bottom. Set aside.

Whisk together lemon juice and 2 tbsp. olive oil. Pour into quart size plastic zip lock bag, and add chicken. Marinate in fridge for 30 to 40 minutes, turning bag occasionally.

While chicken is marinating, combine cornflake crumbs, paprika, parsley, mint flakes, salt and pepper. Place in quart-size plastic zip-lock bag. Remove chicken from marinade (discarding marinade); place chicken breasts in plastic bag with crumbs (one piece at a time) and shake to coat with crumb mixture. Place chicken in prepared baking dish. Sprinkle any remaining crumbs on top of chicken and drizzle each piece with 1/2 tsp. olive oil. Bake for approximately 20 to 25 minutes (or until chicken is white throughout), being careful not to over bake.

Baked Chicken - Italian Style

Source: Lucy Peters

Vicki's note: This recipe is from Grandma Amico. My mom says Grandma would make it as a special dish for company. The chicken would always be fresh from the neighborhood poultry market.

6 boneless and skinless chicken breasts

2 eggs , slightly beaten

1/2 cup milk

1 1/2 cups Italian flavored breadcrumbs

1 1/2 teaspoons dried parsley

1 teaspoon dried mint flakes

1 teaspoon salt

1/4 teaspoon pepper

6 tablespoons butter, melted

6 tablespoons lemon juice, freshly squeezed

Preheat oven to 375 degrees.

Wash chicken, blot dry with paper towels. Set aside.

Mix together milk and eggs in a shallow bowl. Put bread crumbs in a shallow dish or large plastic bag, then add parsley, mint flakes, salt and pepper; mix well. Dip chicken breasts in egg mixture, then in breadcrumb mixture, pressing crumbs to coat all sides. Place in a shallow baking dish which has been sprayed with cooking spray (preferably olive oil spray). Cover with plastic wrap and let set for about 15 minutes. This lets the chicken come to room temperature allowing it cook more evenly and absorb the butter and lemon.

While chicken is resting, combine lemon juice and melted butter. Spoon half of mixture over chicken breasts.

Place in preheated oven and bake for 15 minutes. Spoon remainder of butter/lemon juice mixture over chicken and bake for additional 15-20 min., or until chicken is cooked through. Temperature should be 160 degrees.

Prep Time: 20 minutes   Start to Finish: 1 hour   Servings: 6

Buffalo Chicken Wings
with Blue Cheese Dressing
Source: Vicki McNickle

Vicki's note: Many a cold winter night in Buffalo, we would order a large bucket of wings, pizza, antipasto and just pig out! This was always followed by card playing of course!

4 pounds chicken wings

1 teaspoon salt

1/2 teaspoon black pepper

1/4 cup butter

2 tablespoons hot sauce

1 tablespoon vegetable oil

1 1/2 cups all-purpose flour

Non-stick oil spray

CHICKEN WING SAUCE:

8 tablespoons Louisiana
   hot sauce

8 tablespoons unsalted butter

1 1/2 tablespoons white
   wine vinegar

1/8 teaspoon garlic powder

1/2 teaspoon salt

5 stalks celery, cut into 3" sticks

BLUE CHEESE SAUCE:

6 ounces blue cheese,
   room temperature

4 tablespoons buttermilk

1 cup sour cream

3/4 cup mayonnaise

1 tablespoon white wine vinegar

1/2 teaspoon sugar

1 teaspoon garlic powder

1/2 teaspoon salt

1/4 teaspoon pepper

Preheat oven to 425 degrees. Line 2 rimmed cookie sheets with non-stick aluminum foil or regular aluminum foil sprayed well with oil spray. Set aside.

Cut off excess fat from wings. Rinse under cold water and dry with paper towels completely. Cut wings into 2 pieces. Place in a large bowl. Season with salt and pepper. Add hot sauce and vegetable oil and toss to coat evenly.

Place flour in a large zip-lock bag, add wings in small batches and shake to coat. The wings should be lightly dusted with the flour. Shake excess flour from wings and place on cookie sheets. Spray wings with oil spray. Bake for 20 minutes, turn over and bake for additional 20 minutes, until browned and crusty.

While wings are cooking, make CHICKEN WING SAUCE: Mix all ingredients in a saucepan over low heat. Bring to simmer, stirring occasionally. Turn off heat.

After removing wings from oven, let sit for a few minutes, then transfer to a large bowl or pot. Pour sauce (RECIPE above) over the wings while wings are still hot, and toss with a large spoon to coat completely. Serve with celery sticks and blue cheese dipping sauce (recipe below).

BLUE CHEESE SAUCE

Cream room temperature blue cheese. Add remaining ingredients, stir well. Refrigerate for at least an hour to allow the flavors to meld. Taste; adjust seasonings or add more buttermilk if too thick.

Serving Ideas: Serve warm wings blue cheese dip and celery.

Prep Time: 15 minutes   Start to Finish: 1 hour 30 minutes   Servings: 8

Carol's Marinated Grilled Chicken

Source: Carol Miller

Vicki's note: This is an awesome marinade from my awesome sister-in-law, Carol!

1/2 cup olive oil

1/2 cup cooking sherry

1 large clove garlic, minced

1 tablespoon paprika

2 tablespoons fresh lemon juice

1 teaspoon salt

1/2 teaspoon pepper

4 boneless skinless chicken breasts halves

Mix all marinade ingredients in a medium bowl. Pour over chicken into a 1 quart zip-lock bag and marinate in the refrigerator for four hours. Remove chicken from marinade and place on hot grill (reserve marinade).

Grill chicken until done, basting often with reserved marinade. Discard any leftover marinade.

Prep Time: 5 minutes   Start to Finish: 2 hours 25 minutes   Servings: 4

Chadian Chicken

Source: Peg Miller

Vicki's note: A very special dish from my sister-in-law Peg....what she says about it is: "This is a wonderfully versatile African stew that can be made with any meat and any vegetables as long as the basic greens and seasonings are included. This has been a favorite in our house since I learned it while my parents were in the Peace Corps in Chad, Africa."

4 tablespoons olive oil, separate use

2 1/2 pounds boneless chicken breasts, cut in 1" cubes

2 medium onions, finely chopped

2 carrots, chopped

2 stalks celery, chopped

3 cloves garlic, minced

1 28 oz. can diced tomatoes

1 6 oz. can tomato paste

4 15 oz. cans chicken broth

2 bay leaves

1 tablespoon chili powder

1 tablespoon curry

1/2 teaspoon crushed red pepper (optional)

1 1/2 teaspoons salt

1/2 teaspoon pepper

2 bunches fresh kale , about three cups chopped (see note in directions)

1/2 small head cauliflower, flowerets

1 small head broccoli, flowerets

1 15 oz. can corn, or 1/2 cup frozen

1 15 oz. can peas, or 1/2 cup frozen (optional)

1 15 oz. can garbanzo beans, drained

10 mushrooms, sliced

1 cup peanut butter

8 cups cooked brown rice

On medium high heat, warm up 2 tbsp. of oil in large pot, and brown chicken pieces. Just brown, don't cook all the way through, about 5 minutes. Remove chicken from pot and set aside. Wipe out pot with paper towels.

On medium low heat, heat up remaining 2 Tbsp. oil, then add onion, carrot and celery. Cook until onions are translucent (8-10 minutes), then add garlic and cook one more minute. Add diced tomatoes and paste to pot, along with 3 cups water, and the 3 15 ounce cans chicken broth, and spices. Increase heat to medium high and bring to a boil. Reduce heat and simmer for 15 minutes. Add back chicken, cleaned chopped kale (remove and discard hard stems when cleaning), cauliflower and broccoli flowerets, and all spices. Bring to a boil, reduce heat to a simmer and cover. Continue cooking for 30 minutes, stirring occasionally.

Add corn (drained), peas (drained), garbanzo beans (drained), and sliced mushrooms; simmer for 30 more minutes, stirring occasionally. If stew is too thick, add more water or chicken broth (up to 15 ounces.)

About five minutes before cooking time is complete, thin peanut butter with 1/2 cup hot water, and stir into the pot. Simmer an additional 5 minutes uncovered. Serve over brown rice.

NOTE: If you don't have all these vegetables available, you can substitute others, but the kale is essential. If you use fewer vegetables, eliminate some of the water. You can also use vegetable stock instead of chicken stock in this recipe if desired. It is a good idea if you are having this over brown rice to put the rice on to cook at the same time as you are waiting for the tomatoes and broth to come to a boil so they are all ready at the same time. You can also serve this over cornmeal polenta or mashed potatoes. Peg says the traditional starch this is served over in Africa is something called "Sadza" which is like cornmeal or "Fungi" which is like polenta.

Prep Time: 45 minutes   Start to Finish: 2 hours   Servings: 14

Chicken and Noodles

Source: Julie McNickle

Vicki's note: This recipe is from my sister-in-law Julie. She has made this for years for Kelsey and Kari and they consider it a real treat when Aunt Julie is around and makes it. The tradition is to eat this over mashed potatoes. Not a low carb meal by any means!

3 pound whole chicken

3 cups flour

3 eggs, beaten

2 15 oz. cans chicken broth,

6 cups mashed potatoes

CHICKEN:

Preheat oven to 350 degrees. Clean out giblets, etc. from inside of chicken cavity. Wash chicken, pat dry with paper towels, and generously salt and pepper inside and out. Place chicken on rack in shallow roasting pan. Add 1 1/2 cups of water to pan and roast in oven for 40 to 50 minutes, or until juices run clear.

NOODLES:

While chicken is cooking, make noodles. Measure flour into bowl; make a well in the center and add eggs. With hands, thoroughly mix egg into flour. If dough is "sticky" add a little more flour and mix until you get a ball that can be kneaded.

Turn dough onto well-floured board; knead until smooth and elastic, about 10 minutes. Cover; let rest 10 minutes.

Divide dough into 4 equal parts. Roll dough, 1 part at a time, into paper-thin rectangle, keeping remaining dough covered. Roll rectangle around rolling pin; slip out rolling pin. Cut dough cross-wise into 1/8-inch strips for narrow noodles and 1/4-inch for wide noodles. Shake out strips and place on towel to dry, about 2 hours. When they break they are dry enough to cook. NOTE: If the noodles are not dry enough they won't cook through. While waiting for the noodles to dry is a good time to make your mashed potatoes.

While noodles are drying, remove chicken from the bones of roasted chicken that has been cooled. Put into a bowl and cover until ready to add to the cooked noodles. If not using the same day, store in fridge until ready to use. Some of juices from chicken can be used in place of broth in cans, however, make sure to separate grease from broth first.

BRINGING IT TOGETHER:

Bring broth to rapid boil in large pot. DO NOT ADD WATER TO POT as it will make noodles tough. Once boiling, add noodles a few at a time, stirring gently until all noodles are in broth. Bring to a medium boil and reduce heat.

Cover pot and allow them to cook until tender, about 12 to 15 minutes.

Add cut up chicken to noodles and serve as is or over mashed potatoes.

Prep Time: 1 hour   Start to Finish: 1 hour 30 minutes   Servings: 6

Chicken Cacciatore

Source: Sally Tudini

Vicki's note: This is one of Aunt Sally's famous chicken dishes. You can never eat just one piece!

3 pounds chicken thighs,
   washed and dried

3 1/4 cups flour

2 teaspoons salt, divided use

1 teaspoon pepper, divided use

1/3 cup olive oil, plus 3 Tbsp.

1 medium yellow onion,
   thinly sliced

1 medium green bell
   pepper, thinly sliced

1 pound mushrooms, quartered

1 clove garlic, minced

1 16 oz. can diced tomatoes

1 cup marinara sauce, or
   optionally use 1 cup
   chicken broth

1 cup red wine (optional)

1 1/2 teaspoons dried basil

1 1/2 teaspoons dried parsley

1/4 teaspoon oregano

Wash and dry chicken pieces, set aside. In a shallow dish, combine flour with 1 tsp salt and 1/2 tsp pepper. Coat each piece of chicken with flour mixture. Set aside (to clean dish). You can also put the flour, salt and pepper in a plastic bag and drop a few pieces into bag at a time, shaking bag until chicken is coated.

In a deep frying pan or pot, heat 1/3 cup oil to 375 degrees. Brown chicken a few pieces at a time in hot oil on all sides - about 5 minutes. As pieces are browned, remove from pan and place on paper towels. Do not overcrowd pan or you will steam the chicken and not fry it.

After all chicken has been browned, pour oil in glass dish to be discarded later. Wipe out pan with paper towels. Heat remaining 3 tablespoons olive oil in pan on medium low. Add onion rings, green pepper to pot. Sauté 8 to 10 minutes until onions are translucent. Add mushrooms and cook 5 minutes more. Add garlic and sauté 1 more minute. Stir in diced tomatoes, marinara, red wine, herbs, and remaining 1 tsp. salt, 1/2 tsp pepper, bring to boil. Lower heat to low. Add chicken, cover and simmer 45 to 55 minutes or until chicken is cooked.

Serving Ideas: Serve over pasta, rice or mashed potatoes.

Prep Time: 15 minutes   Start to Finish: 1 hour 15 minutes   Servings: 4

Chicken Cordon Blue

Source: Vicki McNickle

Vicki's note: This is a recipe that my dad (Paul Miller Sr.) used to love. If he was coming to visit, I always made sure to make it. It is now one of Taylor's favorite dishes too, and when he's home from college I try to make sure to make it.

4 half chicken breast,
   skinless and boneless

8 slices deli-style ham slices

8 slices gruyere cheese, or
   Swiss cheese, sliced thin

1/4 cup butter

8 tablespoons fresh lemon juice

1 large egg

4 tablespoons milk, If milk is
   not available, can use water

1 1/2 cups Italian flavored
   breadcrumbs

1/2 teaspoon salt

1/4 teaspoon pepper

2 dozen toothpicks

Preheat oven to 350 degrees.

Rinse chicken breasts under cold water; dry with paper towels. Lay each chicken breast between 2 pieces of wax paper. Using the flat side of a meat mallet, gently pound the chicken to 1/4-inch thickness. Take care not to pound too hard because the meat may tear or create holes. Put on dish to prepare for "assembly". You can also ask your butcher to do this step for you.

Slice ham and cheese into strips about 1 1/2 inches wide - place on a plate to make ready for "assembly". Melt butter in microwave safe dish. Add lemon juice to melted butter and stir to incorporate; set aside. Beat eggs in shallow bowl large enough to accommodate a chicken breast with 4 tablespoons milk. Combine breadcrumbs, salt and pepper in separate shallow dish large enough to accommodate chicken breast. Have a third dish available for "assembly".

Dip each chicken breast in egg, then in breadcrumbs, coating each side and pressing crumbs into breast so they adhere. Put breaded breast on plate, and layer as follows - starting at narrowest end, spread 1/2 tablespoon of melted lemon butter mixture, followed by two to three strips of the ham; finish with two to three strips of the cheese, leaving a 1/2 inch margin on all sides to help seal the roll. Roll up tight like a jellyroll. Squeeze the log gently to seal and secure with toothpicks. If breading fell off a bit during rolling, sprinkle a little more breadcrumbs over top. Place on aluminum foil-lined baking sheet.

Once all rolls are assembled and on sheet, drizzle 1/2 tablespoon of lemon butter mixture over tops of each. Bake in oven for 20 to 25 minutes. Remove from oven, cover with aluminum foil and let sit for five minutes before serving.

Prep Time: 10 minutes   Start to Finish: 45 minutes   Servings: 4

Turkey with Chestnut Stuffing

Source: Vicki McNickle

Vicki's note: This recipe is the one Mom has been making all my life on Thanksgiving. Since my brother Paul and I were younger, we've been the ones given the job of peeling the chestnuts. It's a tedious task that we used to resent, but now we think of as a fond task we get to share. In the past few years we have passed this tradition on to our children, but they don't seem to mind it so much! See additional notes in cookbook on Thanksgiving - this holiday is a big deal in our family!

This recipe has three parts - cooking the giblets to make the stock for the stuffing, making stuffing and cooking the turkey. While making your own broth is not essential (you could use canned broth as a substitute), I have found that it is a very easy to make.

20 pounds Turkey, free range if
   you can get it is very yummy!

STOCK FOR STUFFING

Giblets, neck and livers
   from inside turkey

3 stalks celery

3 medium carrots

2 medium yellow onions

1 tablespoon dried parsley

1 teaspoon salt

1/2 teaspoon pepper

2 teaspoons poultry seasoning

CHESTNUT STUFFING

1 pound chestnuts, or 15oz. jarred can
   also be used to cut down prep time.

2 cups celery, diced (roughly 5-6 stalks)

2 cups yellow onion, diced (2
   large or 3-4 medium)

3/4 cup butter

2 12 oz packages of herb stuffing mix

1/3 cup fresh parsley, chopped,
   or 5 tablespoons dried

1 teaspoon salt

1 teaspoon pepper

Meat from giblets, from above step

2 teaspoons poultry seasoning,
   more if needed

5 cups turkey stock (from prior step)
   or use canned chicken broth

TURKEY

1/4 cup butter, softened

1 teaspoon salt

1/2 teaspoon pepper

Stuffing, recipe above

1 cup white wine (optional) - this is to
   add flavor to the drippings for gravy

STOCK FOR STUFFING AND GRAVY

1 1/2 hours prior to cooking turkey you will want to prepare the stock. This can be done the night before as well, just make sure to re-seal the bag with the turkey completely after removing the giblets, etc. Remove giblets, neck and liver from turkey, rinse under cold water, and place in large pot. Add cold water to the pot to about 3 inches above the giblets, etc. Bring to a boil over high heat. Once boiling add 3 stalks celery, 3 medium carrots and 2 medium onions that have been cut into large chunks, along with 1 tbsp. dried parsley, 1 teaspoons salt, 1/2 teaspoons pepper and 2 teaspoons poultry seasoning. Bring back to a boil, then reduce to a simmer and cook for 45 minutes, stirring occasionally.

Let broth cool until you can handle the giblets, etc. With the exception of the liver (it is usually too bitter to use in the stuffing), remove any meat you can from the meat pieces you cooked in the broth. Set aside. These small pieces of meat will be used in the stuffing. Strain the stock of any other meat or veggies into a large bowl - at this point you have the stock for the stuffing and the gravy. The cooked veggies can now be discarded.

STUFFING

While stock is cooking, prepare your stuffing. If using fresh chestnuts - preheat oven to 425 degrees. "Score" bottom of chestnuts by putting a small slit into the lighter color of nut at bottom. Note: If you don't score, they will "pop" from the pressure in the oven. While this can be exciting, it can also be a bit nerve-racking! Place in one layer on baking sheet, sprinkle with about 1/4 cup water - you just want to give the pan and nuts a little moisture, you are not covering them in water. Use your hand to sprinkle the water over the nuts. Roast in oven 20 to 25 minutes. Remove the nuts from the oven, mound them in an old towel, wrap them up, squeeze them hard -- they should crackle. Let them sit for a few minutes, and once cool enough to handle, remove skin from nuts. You may be able to do this with your hands, or may want to use a small paring knife to help peel the skins off. Chop nuts into 1/2 inch chunks - doesn't have to be exact, just don't chop them too much. You want nice chunks that you will able to taste them in the stuffing. If you don't want to go through this hassle, buy jarred chestnuts.

While the chestnuts are roasting, dice up 2 cups celery and 2 cups yellow onion. In a large pot (big enough to accommodate the two bags of stuffing) melt the 3/4 cup butter over medium heat, then add the onion and celery and sauté until onions are translucent - about 10 to 12 minutes. Remove from heat. Add stuffing, chopped chestnuts and seasoning to pot - mix well. Add the stock slowly mixing well as you add each cup. The stuffing should be moist. If more stock is needed, add a little at a time.

TURKEY

Pre-heat oven to 325 degrees. In an area free of other foods, etc. rinse inside and outside of turkey with cold water. Pat outside dry with paper towels and place on a flat, clean surface. Mix softened butter in small bowl (large enough to get your hand in though) with salt and pepper. Working from the large cavity end, gently run your fingers between the skin and the meat to loosen the skin, taking care not to tear the skin (be careful not to do this with rings on your fingers!). Place the softened butter under the skin and gently massage the skin to spread the butter evenly over the whole breast.

Salt and pepper the inside of bird and stuff the cavity with the stuffing. Leave a little room inside as stuffing will expand a bit during cooking. Truss turkey or, alternatively, tie the legs closed with a strong piece of kitchen twine to assure the stuffing doesn't fall out as the turkey roasts. Place stuffed bird on a rack in roasting pan, tucking the wings underneath to keep them from burning. Place remaining stuffing in an oven- safe bowl to be heated up later. Place extra stuffing in fridge until ready to heat.

Transfer the turkey to a roasting pan, fitted with a roasting rack. Cover the breasts with aluminum foil - tenting loosely. Cook the turkey on lowest rack according to cooking times that came with turkey - usually about 12 minutes per pound (see note below on how to know when the bird is done.) Baste the turkey occasionally during cooking.

In the last hour of cooking add 1 cup of wine if using for gravy recipe. Half an hour before end of cooking time remove the foil so turkey skin will crisp. If any part of the wings or legs begin to burn, cover with a piece of aluminum foil. Half an hour before the bird is done cooking begin making your gravy using the pan drippings. See recipe in book for this.

How do you know when it's done? The temperature of the thigh meat (where the meat is thickest and takes the longest time to cook) should register 165 degrees when tested with an instant-read thermometer. When done, remove the bird from the oven, transfer it to a flat surface (ideally with sides so drippings don't run over), cover with aluminum foil and allow it to rest for 20 minutes before removing the stuffing and carving the meat.

Before carving, remove stuffing to a serving bowl, adding other stuffing you heated in the oven or microwave. Cover to keep warm until ready to serve. After letting turkey rest for 20 minutes, carve turkey and serve with gravy, stuffing and all the other great foods that go with Thanksgiving dinner!

Serving Ideas: See recipe for gravy to serve with turkey, mashed potatoes and stuffing. Jarred chestnuts can be used in place of fresh, and canned chicken broth can be used if you don't want to make your own from turkey innards. See recipe notes on this.

Prep Time: 1 hour   Start to Finish: 4 hours   Servings: 20

Lucy, Tim, Taylor, Vicki, Sandy Amico and Len

Buffalo, NY – July 2007

Avocado & Orange Salad

Source: Virginia Amico

Vicki' note: This is a wonderful summer salad. I remember it was always a treat when mom made this.

1 large orange, sectioned
and cut into 1/2" cubes

2 medium, ripe avocados, sliced
and cut into 1/2" cubes

3 tablespoons orange juice

1 tablespoon olive oil,
or more to taste

1/8 teaspoon garlic powder

1 tablespoon fresh parsley,
chopped fine

1/2 teaspoon salt

1/4 teaspoon pepper

Prepare orange and avocados and place into serving bowl. Set aside.

In a separate small bowl, mix dressing ingredients (orange juice through salt and pepper). Pour dressing over fruit; stir very gently. Allow salad to marinate half hour in refrigerator. Before serving let salad come to room temperature for 15 minutes.

Prep Time: 12 minutes   Start to Finish: 1 hour   Servings: 4

Cucumber and Onion Salad

Source: Shirley McNickle

Vicki's Note: This recipe is a favorite of Tim's - his mom used to make it when he was a kid in the summer time, using homegrown cucumbers and onions.

6 large cucumbers, peeled and thinly sliced

1 large onion, cut in half, thinly sliced

1 1/2 cups water, warm (NOT hot)

3/4 cup sugar

1/2 cup apple cider vinegar

1 teaspoon salt

1/2 teaspoon pepper

Put the sliced cucumber and onion in a container that ideally you can store this salad in the fridge with. Make sure it is large enough for the cucumber, onion AND the liquid. Toss together the onion and cucumber gently.

Mix warm water, apple cider and sugar in bowl. Stir until sugar is melted. Add salt and pepper and pour over cucumber and onion mixture. Gently stir.

Cover container and let sit in refrigerator for at least one hour to let flavors meld. The longer this salad sits, the better it tastes. You can keep this in the fridge for up to a week. You can even add more cucumber and onion if you have left over marinade.

Prep Time: 15 minutes   Start to Finish: 1 hour 15 minutes   Servings: 4

Fennel and Pear Salad

Source: Len & Astrid Amico

1 5 oz package salad
   mix, romaine, butter
   and green lettuce

3 ounces Romano cheese,
   thinly shaved

2 fennel bulbs, core removed
   and thinly sliced

1 large pear, seeded and
   sliced into strips

DRESSING:

1/4 cup olive oil

1 large lemon, juice only

1/2 teaspoon salt

1/4 teaspoon pepper

Place salad greens, cheese, fennel slices and pear strips in chilled bowl. Just before serving salad, in a small bowl whisk together lemon juice and gradually add the olive oil, salt and pepper. Pour dressing over salad and toss gently.

Garbanzo Bean Salad

Source: Lucy Peters

Vicki's note: This is a light and easy salad.

1 16 oz. can garbanzo beans,
    drained and rinsed

1/4 teaspoon garlic powder

1/4 cup Bermuda onion,
    finely chopped

1 tablespoon fresh parsley,
    finely chopped (1 teaspoon
    if using dried)

1/4 teaspoon oregano

1/4 teaspoon Italian seasoning

1 teaspoon salt

1/2 teaspoon pepper

2 tablespoons olive oil

1 tablespoon lemon juice

Combine all ingredients, except olive oil and lemon juice. Cover and refrigerate for about an hour to let flavors meld. Remove from refrigerator, stir gently. Stir in olive oil and lemon juice.

Prep Time: 15 minutes   Start to Finish: 1 hour 15 minutes   Servings: 4

German Potato Salad

Source: Sandy Amico

Vicki's note: Aunt Sandy makes a great potato salad, and she was sweet enough to share the recipe.

6 medium potatoes

1/2 pound bacon

1 medium onion, diced

1/3 cup vinegar

1/3 cup water

1/4 cup sugar

1 teaspoon salt

1/4 teaspoon pepper

1 tablespoon parsley

Peel potatoes, chop into 1 1/2 inch cubes. Place in large pot of cold water (enough to cover potatoes plus 2 inches) along with 1 tablespoon salt. Bring to boil on high heat. Reduce heat to medium and continue cooking until potatoes are soft when fork is inserted into middle (20 to 30 minutes). Drain for about 5 minutes in large colander.

While potatoes are cooking, place strips of bacon in large frying pan and fry until crisp. Remove from pan and drain on paper towels, leaving fat in pan to cook following ingredients.

In the pan with the bacon drippings, brown the onion - but don't burn. Once browned, add the vinegar, water, sugar, salt and pepper. Heat to boiling, then add the potatoes a little at a time, stirring gently. If potatoes are cold when adding, heat thoroughly. Add parsley and bacon, place in a large serving bowl and enjoy!

Serving Ideas: This is an excellent dish to take to picnics as you can serve it piping hot or just a little warm.

Prep Time: 40 minutes   Servings: 8

Green Bean Salad

Source: Lucy Peters

Lucy's note: Grandma used fresh green beans (in season). The almonds are my addition to this wonderful vegetable dish.

1 pound fresh green beans,
 cut diagonally
3 tablespoons olive oil
1 clove garlic, finely minced
1/2 teaspoon salt
1/4 teaspoon pepper
2 tablespoons dried mint flakes,
 or basil if mint is not available
1 1/2 tablespoons red
 wine vinegar
1/4 cup Bermuda onion,
 thinly sliced
1/2 cup slivered almonds, toasted

Put 2 quarts of water on to boil in a large pot. While water is heating, wash green beans, then snap off pointy ends, and cut diagonally in half. When water is at a boil, add green beans and cook for 4 minutes. Drain beans in colander, then rinse with cold water to stop the cooking.

While beans are cooking, blend dressing in a small bow by mixing olive oil, garlic, salt, pepper, mint flakes and vinegar - stir with a whisk to mix all ingredients (or with a fork if you don't have a whisk).

Place well drained beans (if wet, dry off with paper towel) into a salad bowl. Slice onions and add to green beans along with dressing. Mix well. Sprinkle with almonds and serve at room temperature or cold.

Serving Ideas: Serving Ideas: Cubed fresh tomatoes may be added. Broccoli, cauliflower, spinach (fresh, steamed) may be substituted for green beans. Different nuts may be used, i.e., toasted almonds, pine nuts, walnuts. Lemon juice (in place of vinegar) may be used for these vegetables.

Prep Time: 15 minutes   Start to Finish: 40 minutes   Servings: 4

Green Bean Salad with Tomatoes

Source: Virginia Amico

Vicki's note: Aunt Gina introduced this recipe to us last year, and my kids loved it! It is now a favorite at our house.

1 pound fresh green beans

1/4 cup fresh basil, cleaned, dried and sliced into strips

2 tablespoons olive oil

1 tablespoon balsamic vinegar, white is ideal, but red is fine too

1 teaspoon salt

1/2 teaspoon freshly ground black pepper, or to taste

1/2 teaspoon garlic powder, taste salad - you may want more

3/4 cup mozzarella cheese, cut into 3/4" cubes

1 large tomato, cut into 3/4" cubes or 12 cherry tomatoes cut in half

1/4 cup red onion, thinly sliced (optional)

Clean green beans, snapping off ends, then snap in half.

In a large saucepan over medium high heat, bring 2 quarts of water to a gentle boil. Add trimmed green beans and cook, uncovered, 4 to 5 minutes or until crisp-tender (you may need to experiment with the degree of doneness you like). You can also use a vegetable steamer for this if you have one. When checking for doneness they should not be too soft - best if there is a little "crispness" to them. Drain into colander and run tepid water over beans to stop the cooking.

While beans are cooking, wash and cut up tomato, set aside. Cut up mozzarella and onion (if using) set aside.

For salad dressing, whisk olive oil, vinegar, salt, pepper and garlic powder in a small bowl. Toss with green beans after they are well drained and while still a bit warm (not hot). When green beans are cool, add tomato, mozzarella, basil and onion - toss gently one more time. Taste to see if it needs more salt and pepper or garlic powder - this is a personal choice.

Serving Ideas: This salad can be served warm, or stored in fridge until ready to serve. Dress just before serving.

Prep Time: 15 minutes   Start to Finish: 25 minutes   Servings: 4

Macaroni Salad – Lucy's

Source: Lucy Peters

Vicki's note: What would a summer holiday, or picnic be without Mom's famous macaroni salad? Crystal beach, Allegheny Park and lots of fun!! Taylor loves this salad and is always glad when summer comes so I'll make it.

1 pound elbow macaroni

2 small scallions, chopped fine (can also use other small mild onion instead if desired)

2 stalks celery, thinly sliced

2 medium carrots, julienned

3 medium eggs , hard-boiled, (divided use)

1 1/2 tablespoons fresh parsley, 3/4 tbsp. if using dried

1 teaspoon salt

1/2 teaspoon pepper

1 cup mayonnaise

1 tablespoon prepared mustard

paprika, for garnish (optional)

Bring 6 quarts water to boil with one tablespoon salt. If you have not already hard-boiled your eggs, now is a good time to do so.

While water is coming to a boil, julienne carrots, chop celery and onions. Place in large bowl.

Chop TWO of the hard-boiled eggs and put in separate bowl. Set aside 3rd egg in fridge.

Cook macaroni according to package directions. Drain in colander and run under cold water to stop the cooking process and to cool. Drain completely. Add to bowl with vegetables. Stir to combine all ingredients.

In small bowl stir together salt, pepper, parsley, 3/4 cups of mayonnaise and mustard. Pour over macaroni salad mixture and stir to combine. Gently stir in the 2 hard-boiled eggs that have been chopped. Mix well and refrigerate for about two hours to allow flavors to blend and the salad to chill.

Before serving, mix in other 1/4 cup mayonnaise. Slice remaining hard-boiled egg and fan out on top of salad. Sprinkle lightly with paprika,

Serving Ideas: For variation, add 1 can (6 ounces) tuna fish (water packed), rinsed and well drained, added with macaroni.

| Prep Time: 20 minutes | Start to Finish: 2 hours 20 minutes | Servings: 12 |

Macaroni Salad - Carol's

Source: Carol Miller

Vicki's note: From my sister-in-law Carol. She used to make this salad with her Mom, when they lived in Pennsylvania.

1 pound elbow macaroni, I prefer to use Creamette macaroni

8 eggs, hard-boiled (6 chopped; 2 sliced)

1 medium white onion, finely chopped

1 medium cucumber, chopped

6 small sweet pickles, chopped

1 1/4 cups mayonnaise

1 1/2 tablespoons cider vinegar

3 teaspoons sugar

3 tablespoons milk

1/2 teaspoon yellow mustard

1/2 teaspoon salt

1/4 teaspoon black pepper

Bring large pot of water along with 1 tbsp. of salt. Cook macaroni according to package directions. When cooked, rinse with cold water until macaroni is cool.

Transfer macaroni to a large bowl once cooled and add 6 of the chopped hard-boiled eggs, onion, cucumber and sweet pickle.

In a smaller bowl, combine the mayonnaise, vinegar, sugar, milk, mustard, salt and pepper. Mix until well blended. Pour over macaroni mixture and mix well. Add more salt and pepper if desired. Garnish with remaining 2 hard-boiled eggs - sliced on top. Can serve at room temperature or chilled.

Prep Time: 20 minutes   Start to Finish: 40 minutes   Servings: 6

Pasta Salad

Source: Lucy Peters

Vicki's note: Mom made this for us on one of her trips up to San Rafael and we couldn't get enough of it. I have many fond memories of visits with Mom here. She always takes such good care of us and is such a pleasure to have around.

1 pound spiral pasta, or your choice of any small pasta appropriate for cold pasta salad

5 tablespoons olive oil, divided use

1 cup asparagus, cut into 1" pieces

1 package frozen artichoke hearts, cut into quarters

1 cup green peas, frozen, defrosted, uncooked

1/2 green zucchini, peeled and julienned

1 carrot, peeled and julienned

1/2 medium Bermuda onion, or other sweet onion, finely chopped

1/4 cup pine nuts, toasted

1/2 cup black olives, pitted, cut in half

1 tablespoon dried parsley

1 tablespoon dried basil

1/4 teaspoon oregano pinch thyme

2 1/2 tablespoons lemon juice or white wine vinegar

1 teaspoon salt, or more if needed

1/2 teaspoon pepper

1 large tomato, cut into 1" cubes, or one package of grape tomatoes cut in half

Bring a large pot of water to a boil along with one tablespoon salt. While water is coming to a boil clean and cut asparagus, carrots, zucchini, and onion.

Once water comes to a boil, add cut asparagus and cook for 3 minutes. Remove with slotted spoon and put in bowl of cold water with ice cubes to stop cooking. Let pasta water return to a boil.

Place frozen artichoke hearts in layer on paper towels to defrost at room temperature. Cook frozen peas according to package directions.

Cook pasta in boiling water according to package directions, do not overcook. Drain and run under cold water to stop cooking. Drain very well. Toss with 2 tablespoons olive oil to keep pasta from sticking.

In a large bowl combine pasta, vegetables, nuts, olives, herbs and spices. Toss with remaining 3 tablespoons olive oil. Cover and refrigerate for 2 hours or overnight. Remove salad from refrigerator and allow to come to room temperature. Salad will have deeper flavor if allowed to come to room temperature. Just before serving, add lemon juice or vinegar; toss; scatter tomatoes over top.

Serving Ideas: Where recipe calls for julienned you can cut in half and slice thin instead if that is easier for you.

Prep Time: 1 hour   Start to Finish: 1 hour   Servings: 10

Potato Salad

Source: Mary Ann Amico

Lucy's note: This is a wonderful potato salad!

**3 pounds white
potatoes, washed**

1 1/4 cups mayonnaise

1/2 cup milk

1 teaspoon mustard

1 teaspoon salt

1/4 cup green onion, minced

1/4 cup green bell pepper, minced

1/4 cup celery, diced

2 teaspoons dried parsley

1/4 teaspoon garlic powder

**6 eggs, hard-boiled, 3
chopped, 3 sliced**

Place the potatoes and 2 tablespoons of salt in a large pot of water. Cover potatoes with water by about two inches. Bring the water to a boil, then lower the heat and simmer for 10 to 15 minutes, until the potatoes are barely tender when pierced with a knife. Drain the potatoes in a colander, then place the colander with the potatoes over the empty pot and cover with a clean, dry kitchen towel. Allow the potatoes to steam for 15 to 20 minutes.

While potatoes are cooking, whisk together mayonnaise and milk, then add mustard and salt and mix well. Set aside.

When the potatoes are cool enough to handle, cut them into 1 inch cubes. Place the cut potatoes in a large bowl. While the potatoes are still warm, pour enough dressing over them to moisten. Add the bell pepper, celery and green onion, 2 teaspoons of salt, 1 teaspoon pepper, parsley and garlic powder. Toss well with remaining salad dressing. Gently fold in the 3 chopped hard boiled eggs.

Cover, and refrigerate for a few hours to allow the flavors to blend. Gently stir salad upon removing from refrigerator, put sliced remaining 3 hard-boiled eggs on stop. Serve cold or at room temperature.

Serving Ideas: If using russet potatoes you may want to peel them before cooking.

| Prep Time: 30 minutes | Start to Finish: 3 hours | Servings: 8 |

Rice & Kidney Bean Salad

Source: Sally Tudini

4 tablespoons oil

3 tablespoons vinegar

1 1/4 teaspoons dry mustard

1 large garlic clove, crushed

1/2 teaspoon salt

1/4 teaspoon pepper

1 cup brown rice, cooked,
   or white rice, cooked

1 16 oz. can red kidney beans,
   drained and rinsed

1/4 cup red onion, chopped fine

1/4 cup pimiento-stuffed
   green olives, sliced

2 eggs, hard-boiled,
   chopped coarsely

1/2 cup celery, sliced

2 cups lettuce, shredded

1/2 cup sweet green pepper,
   cut into thin strips

In a large bowl, beat oil, vinegar, mustard, garlic, salt and pepper until blended. Add hot rice and toss to blend. Cool to room temperature, add drained and rinsed beans, onion, olives, egg and celery. Toss to blend.

Serve on plate over lettuce and pepper strips

Prep Time: 20 minutes   Start to Finish: 1 hour   Servings: 4

Three Bean Salad

Source: Lucy Peters

1 can kidney beans

1 can cannellini beans

1 can garbanzo beans

1 small Bermuda onion,
   chopped fine

1 medium celery stalk,
   chopped small

1/2 teaspoon salt

1/4 teaspoon pepper

1 teaspoon dried oregano

1 teaspoon dried basil

3 tablespoons olive oil

1 1/2 tablespoons white
   wine vinegar

Drain and rinse beans very well. Place in a large bowl. Add onion, celery, salt, pepper, oregano and basil. Stir gently. Add olive oil and vinegar, and stir gently again. Cover and refrigerate for 2 hours or overnight, let come to room temperature before serving for best flavor. Adjust seasonings, if necessary.

Serving Ideas: This salad is a great lunch time or summer picnic side dish.

Prep Time: 15 minutes   Servings: 8

Tomato Salad

Source: Grandma Amico

Lucy's note: This was a fall season salad in our house. Tomatoes were at their peak flavor then. I could never get enough of this salad when I was growing up. It's still one of my favorites.

**6 medium tomatoes, ripe,
  with some firmness**
1/4 cup olive oil
1 1/2 tablespoons wine vinegar
1 clove garlic, minced
1 1/2 teaspoons dried basil
1/2 teaspoon salt
1/4 teaspoon pepper
**1 tablespoon fresh basil,
  cut into thin strips**

Slice tomatoes 1/4 inch thick. Arrange the tomato slices in slightly overlapping circles on a deep round plate.

Thoroughly combine remaining ingredients in a jar or bowl. Spoon over tomatoes. Sprinkle additional fresh basil on top.

Serving Ideas: Sliced Bermuda onions and sliced cucumbers may be added, (layering with tomatoes). Or omit the cucumbers and use sliced mozzarella cheese, instead.

Back Row: Peg Miller, Bill Suiter, Stan Miller, Carol Miller, Sallyanne Amico, Harry Miller, Roxanne Amico
Front Row: Lucy Peters, Len Miller, Paul Miller, Marianne Amico, Marshall Peters
Las Vegas, NV 1990's (after Uncle Sam's passing)

Sauces

Lucy, Virginia, Cheryl, Len, and Peg
Making of the sauce - Thanksgiving week, 2004

Aglio e Olio Sauce

Olive Oil Sauce

Source: Lucy Peters

Lucy's note: This recipe is from Grandma Amico. This was a quick Friday night pasta dish during Lent season.

1/2 cup olive oil

4 cloves garlic, chopped

1 tablespoon fresh parsley,
   finely chopped

1 teaspoon salt

1/2 teaspoon pepper

1/4 cup pine nuts, lightly
   toasted (optional)

1 pound spaghetti,
   cooked al dente

Romano cheese, or Parmesan

On high heat, bring large pot of water and 1 tablespoons salt to boil to cook pasta according to package directions.

While pasta is cooking heat olive oil in small pot on low heat. Stir in garlic and cook for 1 minute. Remove from heat and add parsley, salt, pepper and pine nuts - set aside.

Once pasta is cooked, drain, reserving about 2 cups of cooking water. Add cooking water, a little at a time to garlic mixture. Mix sauce with the cooked pasta in a large serving bowl. Serve with grated Romano cheese on the side.

Serving Ideas: Can use other types of pasta for this dish as well

Prep Time: 15 minutes   Start to Finish: 20 minutes   Servings: 4

Eggplant Sauce (Pasta all Norma)

Source: Lucy Peters

Lucy's note: When we were in Sicily in 2007, Uncle Ange fell in love with this pasta dish (which is very popular in Sicily). The recipe has been added to recall our days in Sicily.

2 small to medium eggplants, cut into 2-inch pieces

2 tablespoons olive oil

1/2 medium onion, chopped fine

2 cloves garlic, chopped fine

1 28 oz can crushed tomatoes, plus 1/2 can water

1 tablespoon dried basil, or 2 tablespoons fresh

1 teaspoon salt

1/2 teaspoon pepper

1 pound rigatoni pasta, or to your liking

6 tablespoons ricotta Salada, coarsely grated (divided use) NOTE: if you cannot find ricotta Salada, then Romano or Parmesan cheese can be substituted.

Bring 6 quarts of water to which 1 tablespoon of salt has been added, to a boil.

While water is coming to a boil, wash, dry and peel eggplant. Cut into 2 inch pieces and place in colander - try to have one layer if possible. Sprinkle with 1 Tbsp salt and toss to coat eggplant. Let eggplant sit in colander for 30 minutes - try to keep separate if possible. This lets the bitterness come to the surface and is washed off in the next step. Rinse well with cold water, drain and wipe dry. Set aside.

In a saucepan, heat olive oil over medium low heat. Add onions and sauté until translucent, 4 to 5 minutes. Add garlic, sauté for 1 more minute. Add the eggplant and cook, stirring often until softened and lightly browned, about 8 to 10 minutes. Add can of tomatoes, 1/2 cup water, basil (NOTE: If using fresh basil, add in the last five minutes of cooking), salt and pepper; bring to boil. Reduce heat and simmer sauce for 30 minutes.

12 minutes before sauce is done cooking, add rigatoni to boiling water and cook per package directions. Drain pasta well and pour into pot with the now fully cooked eggplant sauce (heat should be off). Add 4 tablespoons of ricotta salada to pan and stir well. Put into individual bowls or put all pasta and sauce into large serving bowl. Serve with extra ricotta salada.

| Prep Time: 20 minutes | Start to Finish: 1 hour 10 minutes | Servings: 6 |

Turkey Gravy

Source: Vicki McNickle

Vicki's note: Thanksgiving is the "big event" in our family. There are certain tasks we each have, and for years now, one of mine has been making gravy. It has become the tradition that EVERYONE in my family deems it necessary to contribute their opinions and thoughts about how I should be making the gravy - offering unsolicited advice all the way through the process. By this time in the day, it is likely we have already begun doing shots of tequila and drinking beer, thus it can be even all that more entertaining when people are offering advice!

Drippings from roast turkey
6 tablespoons fat from turkey drippings, or 6 tablespoons butter
4 tablespoons flour
1 1/2 cups white wine, separate use
6 cups chicken broth, or broth you made with giblets
1 teaspoon salt
1/2 teaspoon pepper

In the last hour of cooking turkey add 1 cup of white wine to pan. A half hour before the turkey is to be taken from the oven, remove the drippings from the bottom of the pan with a baster.

Let drippings rest in a heatproof bowl and let rest while fat separates from juice. Once separated, ladle the fat that has floated to the top into a gravy separator and let sit a bit until grease has settled to the top. Once it has, pour off the broth and put the fat into a separate bowl. Repeat with remaining drippings. If you do not have a gravy separator, use a spoon and gently scoop the grease off the top of the bowl of drippings.

Heat a medium large pot on medium heat. Add 6 tablespoons of grease from drippings and let heat up for about a minute (if using butter, let it melt), then add flour stirring constantly with a wooden spoon. Mixture should be a liquid paste. If too thick, add more grease. If too thin, add a bit more flour - it should be a bit pasty. Stir on low heat 8 to 10 minutes - don't let mixture burn. You want to let it cook a while to cook the flour. This makes the "roux" base for your gravy.

Measure out 6 cups of drippings, using giblet or chicken broth needed to make 6 cups. Add the liquid to the roux a little at a time, mixing with wire whisk to incorporate broth into roux, making sure to eliminate any lumps. Once all broth is incorporated, add remaining 1/2 cup wine, salt and pepper. Bring broth to a boil, lower heat, and simmer for fifteen to twenty minutes. If not ready to serve, cover pot and reheat when ready to serve.

Prep Time: 1 hour   Start to Finish: 1 hour

Marinara Sauce

Source: Lucy Peters

Lucy's note: This is a quick, delicious sauce. Grandma cooked this sauce quite often. Sometimes she would hard-boil some eggs and serve them (quartered) alongside the pasta or alone with this sauce over the top.

1 1/2 tablespoons olive oil

1 medium yellow onion, finely chopped

2 cloves garlic, minced

1 small carrot, peeled and cut into 4 pieces

2 28 oz. cans crushed tomatoes

1/2 teaspoon salt

1/4 teaspoon black pepper

1 teaspoon sugar

2 tablespoons fresh basil, chopped or 1 1/2 teaspoon dried

1 1/2 teaspoons butter

Heat oil in medium pot over medium heat. Add onion; sauté until translucent 8 to 10 minutes. Add garlic; continue sautéing for 1 more minute. Add crushed tomatoes, salt, pepper, carrot and sugar. NOTE: If using dried basil, add at this time also. Bring sauce to a boil, then reduce heat to simmer.

Cook over low heat for 40 minutes. About 5 minutes before finishing, stir in 1 1/2 teaspoon butter and fresh basil (if using)

Serving Ideas: Enjoy over any type of pasta you like. It can also be used in some casseroles and soups, or as an addition to some vegetables.

Prep Time: 15 minutes   Start to Finish: 1 hour   Servings: 4

Spaghetti Sauce with Meatballs

Source: Lucy Peters

Vicki's note: This is Grandma Amico's recipe. Whenever I smell sauce cooking I'm brought back to the smells of Grandma's kitchen as a little girl. When you walked in, the smell permeated the house. And oh what a wonderful smell it was. The next thought I have is Mom making sauce on Sunday mornings in our house. It was a wonderful smell to wake up to.

Lucy's notes: Serve sauce over any favorite pasta with plenty of Romano cheese and good Italian bread. Note: This recipe can be easily doubled or tripled. Sauce freezes very well. If meat and/or meatballs have been used, store or freeze leftovers separately from sauce. Reheat meatballs separately (with a little sauce added). (Meatballs can become "rubbery" if overcooked).

1 pound beef chuck (optional)
   cut into 1" cubes
1/2 pound pork (optional)
   cut into 1" cubes
4 tablespoons olive
   oil, divided use
1 medium yellow onion,
   finely chopped
2 cloves garlic, minced
1 28 oz. can tomato puree
2 28 oz. cans crushed tomatoes
2 tablespoons tomato paste
1 1/2 teaspoons salt
3/4 teaspoon black pepper
1 teaspoon sugar
1 tablespoon dried basil

1 large carrot, peeled and
   chopped into 3 chunks
2 tablespoons butter

Meatballs, see note below
   and recipe in book

If adding OPTIONAL meat to recipe (chunks of meat - I'm not talking about meatballs), add 2 Tbsp. olive oil to large heated pot on med-high heat. Add meat in batches and brown - remove to separate bowl once browned on all sides.

Once meat is all browned and removed from pan, reduce heat to medium low and add 2 tbsp. olive oil to pan - let oil heat up slightly. Add onion and cook until translucent, about 8 to 10 minutes. Add garlic and cook for one minute more. Add tomato puree and crushed tomatoes (NOTE: If you don't like chunks of tomatoes, puree tomatoes in blender before adding). Stir in tomato paste. Add 1/2 cup hot tap water, salt, pepper, sugar, carrots and dry basil (if using fresh add during last 15 minutes of cooking). Bring to low boil, then lower heat to simmer. Continue simmering over very low heat for 1 1/2 to 2 hours stirring often. You will want to put a lid slightly over pot, but not fully covering - letting steam escape. If you keep a tight lid on sauce it will become too watery and will give it a bitter taste. Stir sauce often during cooking. About 15 minutes before sauce is finished add butter - stir in until melted. Do this before you add the meatballs?

Meatballs add a great flavor to sauce. After putting together sauce and letting it start to simmer, combine meatball mixture (see recipe in book) and put in refrigerator for about an hour so flavors meld. About 45 minutes before sauce is finished cooking, roll your meat-balls into 2 to 3 inch balls. Broil on second rack in oven below broiler until lightly browned (use an aluminum foil-lined broiler pan) about 5 minutes. Turn and continue cooking 5 min-utes on other side. If you have meat in sauce, remove the meat to a separate bowl before adding meatballs. Add meatballs to sauce in the last 1/2 hour of cooking. GENTLY stir into sauce, making sure not to break up meatballs.

Tomato Basil Sauce

Source: Lucy Peters

Vicki's note: Mom found this recipe in her travels a few years ago and passed it along to me. This is simple and wonderful - a very quick sauce, easy to make on a busy weekday.

6 large tomatoes, or 28 oz. can crushed tomatoes

2 tablespoons olive oil

3 cloves garlic, minced

1/2 teaspoon salt

1/4 teaspoon pepper

6 large basil leaf, cleaned, dried and cut into 1 inch strips

1/8 teaspoon crushed red pepper flakes

Bring large pot of water to boil. While water is heating up, wash tomatoes and score the bottom in a cross. When water is boiling, add tomatoes and blanch for 8 minutes. Remove from water and place in bowl of cold water. When tomatoes are cool enough to handle, remove skins. If using canned tomatoes this step can be skipped.

In a blender or Cuisinart chop tomatoes.

In a medium sauce pan, heat oil on medium, add garlic and sauté for 1 minute, then add tomatoes, salt and pepper. Cook for about 20 minutes, stirring occasionally. Chop basil and add to sauce with remaining crushed red pepper. Continue cooking for 15 to 20 minutes. Serve over linguini or any pasta you like.

Prep Time: 10 minutes   Start to Finish: 50 minutes   Servings: 2

Marianne Giambroni, Cynthia Start, Harry Miller, Taylor Suiter, Vick McNickle,
Lucy Peters, Peg Miller
San Diego, CA in mid 1990's

Harry & Kelly Machnov with Lucy
San Rafael, CA 2009

Seafood

Lucy & Vicki

Palermo, Sicily Italy 2004

This was Mom's and my first trip to Italy.

The home where Grandma (Marianna Amico) was born and her mother Rosaria

Vaccalluzza lived.

Calamari (Baby Squid) in Tomato Sauce

Source: Mary Ann Amico

Lucy's note: When Grandma Amico made this, she added fresh green peas to the sauce. Alternative is 1 package frozen green peas added during last 5 minutes of cooking.

5 pounds squid (calamari)

2 tablespoons lemon juice

4 tablespoons olive oil, divided use

2 small yellow onions, finely chopped

4 cloves garlic, minced

1 28 oz. can crushed tomatoes

1 1/4 cups water

1 1/2 teaspoons sugar

1 teaspoon Italian seasoning

1 tablespoon basil

salt and pepper, to taste

Rinse squid several times in very cold water. Remove any membrane that may still be inside cylinder of body meat. Cut flat part of squid into rings. Tentacles may be left whole or cut into pieces. Last rinse should be in cold water to which has been added the 2 tbsp. lemon juice. Drain and pat dry with paper towels.

In a medium pot, heat 2 tbsp. olive oil on medium high heat. Add calamari and sauté in pan for 2 1/2 min. (NO LONGER OR THE CALAMARI WILL BECOME TOUGH AND DRY DURING ADDITIONAL COOKING IN SAUCE). Set aside.

In same pot, heat remaining 2 tablespoons olive oil over medium heat. Sauté onion until translucent - about 5 minutes. Add garlic and sauté 1 minute. Add tomatoes and seasonings. Add the water, adjust heat to low and simmer for 1 hour. Add squid and simmer for an additional 15 minutes. Remove from heat. Serve with lots of crusty Italian bread. Can be also served over linguini and sprinkled with Romano cheese. MMMMM!

Prep Time: 40 minutes

Servings: 8

Cioppino

Italian Fish Stew
Source: Lucy Peters / Vicki McNickle

Vicki's note: Cioppino is one of my favorite dishes! It takes some time to make, but for a great Sunday meal, it's worth it. An important thing to remember in making this is to add the ingredients in the order given and DO NOT OVER COOK! The recipe calls for using cooked crab. If you get fresh, clean it, then cook in a large pot of boiling salted water separately.

1 tablespoon olive oil

1 medium onion, finely chopped

3 cloves garlic, minced

1 tablespoon dry basil

   pinch thyme

pinch oregano

pinch marjoram

1/4 teaspoon crushed

   red pepper flakes

salt and pepper, freshly ground

1/2 cup red wine

1/2 cup white wine

1 cup clam juice

1 28 oz. can plum

   tomatoes, chopped

1 15 oz. can tomato puree

1 pound sea bass steak, cubed

8 sea scallops

8 jumbo shrimp, uncooked,

   peeled and deveined

1 whole Dungeness crab,

   cooked, cleaned well and

   the main body cut into

   four pieces (see note)

8 mussels in shells, well

   scrubbed and debearded

16 littleneck clams in shells,

   well scrubbed

Heat oil over medium heat in a large pot. Add onions and sauté until translucent, 8 to 10 minutes. Add garlic and sauté for 1 minute. Add herbs, spices, wine, and clam juice. Lower heat to low and simmer for 10 minutes. Add tomatoes and tomato puree; simmer for additional 40 minutes.

While sauce is cooking, clean clams and mussels. If you are going to serve Cioppino over pasta, now is a good time to put water on to boil as well. When you begin adding fish in next step to pot of sauce that is a good time to cook your pasta per package instructions.

Once sauce is cooked you are ready to add the seafood. Add in order listed as each seafood cooking time varies. Add cubed sea bass first, simmer 3 minutes. Add scallops next, simmer 3 minutes. Add shrimp next, simmer 2 minutes. Add cooked crab pieces to pot. Stir to incorporate. Place mussels and clams on top of all. Cover pot and steam until mussels and clams are opened (3 to 5 minutes).

NOTE: DISCARD ANY MUSSELS AND/OR CLAMS THAT DO NOT STEAM OPEN! If they don't open this means they are bad and should not be eaten. Remove mussels and clams, set aside. Distribute other seafood evenly into four deep bowls; top with broth, then mussels and clams. If serving with pasta, put drained pasta in bowls first, then top with sauce and fish.

Serving Ideas: Lucy: Serve with crusty French or Italian bread to "sop up" the wonderful broth. You can also add Parmesan cheese on top for an added treat! Although it is not customary to serve grated cheese with seafood, some people like it!

Vicki: My brother Paul and I have made this dish a few times together, and his alternative to this traditional recipe is as follows: Grill fish first before adding to sauce. Steam clams until just opened in 1 bottle clam juice, 1 cup white wine, 2 tbsp parsley, 1/4 cup lemon juice. Place cooked fish in sauce just to heat through before serving. Add clams on top. For a different variation, add 2 links of sweet Italian sausage that have been grilled just with the fish to the sauce.

Prep Time: 45 minutes   Start to Finish: 1 hour 45 minutes   Servings: 4

Crab Meat Fondue

Source: Diane Boney

Vicki's note: This is not on the low-cal dieter's menu; but this is a great fondue. Great for company! Mom got this recipe from her dear friend, Diane Boney.

WHITE SAUCE

2 tablespoons butter

2 tablespoons flour

1 cup milk

FONDUE

1 1/2 cups sharp cheddar cheese, shredded

3/4 teaspoon garlic powder

1/2 teaspoon pepper

1 teaspoon parsley flakes

1/4 cup white wine

1 1/2 cups crab meat, cooked (fresh or frozen)

1/4 cup tiny shrimp, cooked (optional)

1 loaf French bread, cut into 1" cubes (or Italian)

Before making white sauce, it is a good idea to have your cheese shredded and ready to add to white sauce when the time comes.

In a medium sauce pan, melt butter on low heat. Add flour to butter, and stir for about 4 minutes - allowing the flour to fully incorporate and cook into the butter. Slowly add milk, stirring with wooden spoon or whisk as you go. When mixture has begun to thicken, continue stirring for about another 1 minute.

Add shredded cheese and spices. When cheese has melted, add wine, crab meat, and shrimp (if using). Simmer on low heat just until heated through (5 to 8 minutes). While fondue is cooking, cut bread into cubes. Cover bread and set aside.

Serve in fondue pot (if available) over very low flame. Serve with bread cubes.

Serving Ideas: If eating as a meal, serve with salad.

Prep Time: 20 minutes   Start to Finish: 30 minutes   Servings: 8

Fish "Stew"

Source: Lucy Peters

Vicki's note: If you like cioppino you will like this stew. It is very tasty and easy to make. I like it without the olives, which is why I've made it optional here.

2 tablespoons olive oil

3 garlic cloves, minced

1 onion, diced

1 can anchovy fillets, 2 oz. can

1 tablespoon capers,
**   rinsed and drained**

10 kalamata olives, pitted
**   and cut in half (optional)**

1 28 oz can crushed tomatoes

pinch red pepper flakes

salt and pepper, to taste

1 teaspoon dried parsley

1 tablespoon dried basil
**   fresh lemon juice (from**
**   1 large lemon)**

2 12 oz bottles clam juice

1 cup white wine

1 pound firm white fish
**   (cut into large cubes)**

Heat olive oil in large pan, over medium heat. Add onion, sauté until translucent; add garlic, sauté for 1 minuter. Add the anchovies and stir continuously until they are "melted" (some small chunks will remain). Add capers and sauté mixture for about 2 minutes; add olives, sauté all ingredients for another 2 minutes. Add crushed tomatoes, red pepper flakes, salt and pepper, parsley and basil. Lower heat and simmer mixture for about 30 minutes.

Add lemon juice, clam juice and wine. Stir well and continue to simmer over low heat for about 1 1/2 to 2 hours, stirring occasionally. Just before serving, add fish and allow to simmer for 8 to 10 minutes (depending on thickness of fish). Serve over cooked rice, risotto or linguini.

Serving Ideas: NOTES: Go very light on the addition of salt because of the saltiness of the anchovies, olives and capers!

1) Frozen cooked shrimp may be substituted for white fish. If using shrimp, reduce simmer time to 2 minutes after adding to sauce.

2) A combination of white fish and cooked shrimp may also be used. If doing this, add shrimp during last 2 minutes of simmer time.

3) Try to cook only as much fish and/or shrimp as will be used during that meal. Fish and seafood gets very tough when reheated.

4) Leftover sauce can be frozen (without fish). Add 1 bottle more clam juice to defrosted sauce (while it's reheating) and serve over cooked linguine.

Prep Time: 20 minutes   Servings: 4

Italian Fisherman's Salad

Source: Lee Ann Giglio

Vicki's note: My dear friends Vinny & Lee Ann Giglio contributed this recipe. Though not related by blood, they are as close as any family could be.

1 cup mayonnaise

1 package Italian salad
   dressing, dry mix

1 cup buttermilk

1/2 pound vermicelli

1 cup celery, thinly sliced

1/4 cup sweet green
   pepper, chopped

2 eggs, hard-boiled and chopped

1 tablespoon pimientos, chopped

12 ounces medium shrimp,
   cooked (can use fresh as
   well - see note below)

1 teaspoon salt

1/2 teaspoon pepper

1/2 cup almonds, slivered
   and toasted

Make dressing first by combining dry Italian dressing mix and 1 cup mayonnaise. Add 1 cup buttermilk and stir until smooth consistency. Chill for one hour or overnight if possible.

Bring large pot of salted water to boil for cooking pasta.

NOTE: If using fresh shrimp, put another pot of water to boil for cooking shrimp. Peel and devein shrimp. Bring water to a boil and cook shrimp for 3 to 8 minutes depending on size. Shrimp will turn pink on the outside and the middle part will be white.

When pasta water comes to a boil, break pasta into bite sized pieces, add to pot of boiling water and cook according to package instructions. Drain well in strainer, running cold water over the pasta to stop cooking. Let pasta cool completely.

While pasta is cooking, chop celery, green pepper, eggs, and pimientos and put in large bowl. Once pasta is cooled mix in with vegetables. Toss with 1/2 of dressing, chill for 2 hours. Just before serving, add remaining dressing, salt and pepper, shrimp and almonds, toss.

Prep Time: 35 minutes   Start to Finish: 45 minutes   Servings: 8

Linguini & Clams

Source: Vicki McNickle

Vicki's note: This recipe is a combination of Mom's and my recipes. Traditional Italian linguini and clams does not have onion or white wine, but I really like this addition.

2 tablespoons olive oil

1/2 medium onion, finely chopped (optional)

3 cloves garlic, minced

1/3 cup white wine

1 8 ounce bottle clam juice

2 tablespoons lemon juice, fresh is best

2 6 oz. cans chopped clams, reserve liquid

1 10 oz. can baby clams, liquid reserved (or 2 more cans of chopped clams)

3 tablespoons fresh parsley, or 1 tablespoon dried

1/2 teaspoon salt

1/4 teaspoon pepper

1/4 teaspoon crushed red pepper

1 pound linguini, or other pasta of your choice

4 tablespoons Romano cheese, grated

Put a large pot of water on to boil, with 1 tablespoon salt.

Heat olive oil over low heat in a medium sauce pan. Add onion (if using) and sauté until translucent. Add garlic; sauté for 1 minute more - do not brown. Add juice from canned clams, bottled clam juice, white wine and lemon juice. Lower heat and simmer sauce for 15 to 20 minutes. NOTE: If using dried parsley, add it to the clam juice at this time.

Water should be boiling by this point. Add pasta and cook per package instructions until al dente. Drain, reserving 2 cups of the cooking water.

Once you have added pasta to the boiling water, add clams, parsley and seasonings to clam juice; simmer until pasta is cooked. Remove from heat. Plate pasta and top with some of the sauce and some of the reserved cooking water (if desired). Alternately, mix sauce in pot with drained pasta, add some of the reserved water, if desired, then plate. Serve cheese on the side

Serving Ideas: Do not use minced clams in this dish - it's just not the same. Also, spend the few extra dollars on good canned clams - they really do taste better. You can also steam 4 pounds of clams in the broth above, using one additional bottle of clam juice. If you choose to do this, make sauce as above, bring to boil, add fresh (scrubbed and cleaned) clams to pot, cover and let them steam for 10 minutes. Add 1/4 cup of melted butter and other spices and parsley, toss and serve sauce and clams over linguini.

Prep Time: 10 minutes   Start to Finish: 40 minutes   Servings: 4

Pasta Con Le Sarde (scratch)

Pasta with Sardines

Source: Vicki McNickle

Vicki's note: a few years back when I couldn't find canned con sarde sauce, I went about finding a recipe I could make from scratch. This recipe is a combination of a few recipes I found and the traditional recipe from my mom and grandmother. I really like the freshness of the ingredients, and it has a slightly different flavor that is a nice change.

1/4 cup olive oil

1 tablespoon butter

2 large fennel bulbs, greens removed and reserved, cores removed and bulbs cut into strips

1 1/2 medium onion, minced

2 – 2 Oz. canned anchovies, boneless

4 – 4 Oz. canned boneless sardines in oil

1 28 Oz. whole tomatoes, chopped

3/4 cup water

3 tablespoons dried currants, or raisins, soaked and drained

2 tablespoons capers, rinsed

1/4 cup pine nut, lightly toasted

4 tablespoons fennel fronds, from reserved bulbs

1 teaspoon dried basil

1 teaspoon salt

1/2 teaspoon pepper

7 saffron threads, or powder (can leave out if you don't have it)

1 pound linguine

1 tablespoon olive oil

1 tablespoon butter

3/4 cup Italian bread crumbs

1/4 cup Romano cheese, grated

Heat olive oil and butter in a large, uncovered, wide pan on medium high heat. Add the sliced fennel and onions and stir to coat with olive oil. Stir frequently and after 10 minutes, sprinkle the onions and fennel with 1 tsp. salt. Lower the temperature to medium. Cook for another 30 minutes, stirring occasionally.

Add boneless anchovies to pot and break up slightly. Anchovies will 'melt' as they heat up - chunks will be left. Cook for about 5 minutes. Add chopped tomatoes, water, currants, capers, fennel fronds, basil, salt, pepper and saffron threads (if using). Bring sauce to a boil, then reduce heat to a simmer. Cook for 20 minutes. Add pine nuts and sardines, break up sardines slightly (you want to leave some chunks) and continue cooking 15 more minutes. If sauce becomes too thick, add a little of the pasta cooking water.

While sauce is cooking, bring 6 quarts of water to which 2 tablespoons of salt have been added, to boil. Cook pasta according to package directions. Reserve 2 cups of cooking water.

While water is heating up and sauce is cooking, prepare breadcrumbs. In a medium frying pan, heat 1 tbsp. oil and 1 tbsp. butter on med-low heat. Add breadcrumbs, and stirring constantly, cook until lightly browned. Remove from heat and set aside. When crumbs are completely cooled, mix in 1/4 cup Romano cheese.

Serve pasta topped with 1/4 cup of the pasta water, 1/2 cup sauce, and bread crumb/cheese mixture on the side.

Prep Time: 20 minutes   Start to Finish: 1 hour   Servings: 4

Pasta Con Le Sarde Sauce (white)

Source: Lucy Peters

Lucy's note: When we were in Sicily in 2007, we were served this version of pasta con le sarde and fell in love with it. It has a unique flavor, making the mouth say "... more, more". Because fennel (or anise) grows wild in Sicily this dish is very popular.

1 pound linguini or spaghetti
1 large fennel bulb, including
    green part and fronds
5 3.75 oz cans sardines,
    skinned and boned
OR 2 pounds fresh sardines,
    filleted and opened
    flat see note below
1 medium onion, finely chopped
6 anchovy fillets, or a 2oz.
    can of filleted anchovy
2/3 cup toasted pine nuts
6 tablespoons capers,
    soaked in hot water for
    5 minutes and drained
7 tablespoons white
    raisins, optional
salt and pepper, to taste
1/2 tablespoon butter
1/2 tablespoon olive oil
1 cup Italian flavored
    breadcrumbs

Clean fennel by removing and discarding the roots and any discolored fronds. Rinse a few times and set aside. Bring a large pot with 5 quarts of lightly salted (1 tablespoon) water to a boil, add fennel and cook, keeping pot at a medium heat for 15 minutes or until fennel is very tender. Scoop out the boiled fennel with a slotted spoon and when cool, chop very fine. Save the fennel water for cooking the pasta.

Drain the sardines, remove from tin. Set aside. If using fresh sardines: Add 3/4 of the sardines with the onion, anchovies, etc. Dip remaining sardines in milk, then in seasoned flour; fry in olive oil. Use to garnish plated pasta.

In a saucepan, sauté onion for about 7 minutes; add anchovies. Continue cooking and stirring - mashing anchovies with a fork until they dissolve after heated through a bit. Add pine nuts, capers, raisins (if using), chopped fennel fronds and sardines. Season with salt and pepper to taste. Add about 1 cup of the reserved water you cooked the fennel fronds in. Cover and simmer, stirring occasionally, for about 25 minutes.

While sauce is cooking, bring remaining fennel water to boil. Add pasta and cook per package directions. When cooked, reserve 1 1/2 cups of the water, and drain pasta.

While pasta and sauce are cooking, heat oil and butter in a medium frying pan medium low heat until butter is melted. Add breadcrumbs and stir constantly until lightly browned - watch carefully as they will burn easily. Set aside.

Pasta and sauce may be combined, or pasta may be plated individually, topped with some of the sauce, and some of the reserved pasta water if desired. Serve with toasted breadcrumbs to sprinkle over top.

Prep Time: 15 minutes   Start to Finish: 45 minutes   Servings: 4

Pasta Con Le Sarde Sauce (Traditional Family Recipe)

Source: Lucy Peters

Vicki's note: Grandma Amico brought this recipe with her when she immigrated from Sicily to the United States in 1928. It is a dish that Taylor loves, and is usually on the list of requested meals when he comes home from college.

3 tablespoons olive
   oil, divided use
1 medium onion, finely chopped
2 cloves garlic, minced
1/2 medium fennel bulb,
   core removed, rinsed and
   finely chopped (reserve
   fronds for later use)
1 2 oz. can boneless
anchovies, drained (see
   note if bones still in)
1 4 oz. can boneless, skinless
   sardines, drained (see note)
2 tablespoons fennel fronds,
   finely chopped (from
   bulb used above)
1 28 oz. can crushed tomatoes
1 1/2 teaspoons dried basil
1/2 teaspoon salt
1/2 teaspoon pepper
1 tablespoon capers,
   rinsed and drained

1 15 oz. can pasta con sarde sauce mix,
   (can be purchased at Italian market)
1/4 cup pine nuts, toasted
1 tablespoon butter
Italian bread crumbs, can use plain
   if you don't have Italian flavored
1 pound pasta, linguini or
   thin spaghetti

In a medium pan heat 2 tablespoons of olive oil over medium heat, add onion and fennel bulb, sauté until onion is translucent, 8 to 10 minutes. Add garlic and sauté for 1 minute more. Reduce heat to medium low and add anchovies to pot. Cook and stir until anchovies have somewhat "melted" into the onion - about 5 minutes. You will still see pieces. Add sardines. Cook and stir over low heat for 5 minutes. Add tomatoes, basil, fennel fronds, salt and pepper. Simmer over low heat for 40 minutes, stirring occasionally. Add Con Sarde sauce and capers. Simmer an additional 15 to 20 minutes. Taste at this point and add additional salt, if needed. Add toasted pine nuts last, just before serving.

While the sauce is simmering, toast the crumbs in a medium frying pan in which you've heated (at medium low heat) the remaining 1 tablespoon of olive oil and1 tablespoon butter. Stir continuously to avoid scorching the crumbs.

Bring pasta water (to which 1 tablespoon of salt has been added) to a boil. Add pasta and cook per package directions. Once cooked, remove 2 cups of the cooking water; set aside. Drain pasta and serve with Con Sarde over top. If sauce is too thick, stir in some of the pasta water before placing on top of the pasta. Serve the breadcrumbs and if desired Romano cheese at the table and allow your guests to help themselves to these toppings.

Serving Ideas: NOTE: If your cans of sardines still have bones in them, remove bones before adding to the pot. This can be accomplished simply by pulling apart gently with your hands and removing the bones.

Prep Time: 15 minutes   Start to Finish: 1 hour   Servings: 4

Pasta with Tuna Sauce

Source: Lucy Peters

Vicki's note: Mom says that when she and my uncles were children, Grandma used to make this sauce on Fridays, using fresh tuna steaks.

1 pound spaghetti, thin or angel hair is best

8 cups marinara sauce, from recipe in book or a jar

1 1/2 pounds tuna steak, cut into chunks, or 4 cans white albacore tuna

Bring large pot of water to boil. Cook pasta according to package directions.

While cooking pasta, heat marinara sauce in medium sauce pan on low heat.

While sauce is heating up, sear tuna in small amount of hot olive oil in large pan on medium high heat. IF USING CANNED TUNA: Drain tuna; add to sauce and simmer just until tuna is heated through. Add tuna to hot marinara sauce; simmer over low heat for about 10 minutes.

Drain pasta. Plate and pour sauce over individual plates.

Prep Time: 15 minutes   Start to Finish: 35 minutes   Servings: 6

Salmon Patties

Source: Carol Miller

Lucy's note: These are great! Jason (Miller) Paul's son, my grandson, Vicki's nephew, loves these patties!

1 16 oz. can salmon,
   boned and skinned

1/4 pound saltine crackers,
   finely crushed

1 small yellow onion, diced

1 egg

1/4 cup milk

1 tablespoon tarragon

1/2 teaspoon salt

1/4 teaspoon pepper

1/4 cup cooking oil

Drain salmon, reserving liquid in a medium bowl. Place salmon in a separate shallow bowl. Remove any residual skin and bones. Break up salmon with a fork; add to reserved liquid and set aside.

In another bowl beat together egg and milk. Mix in crackers, onion, tarragon, salt and pepper. Do not mix ingredients until ready to fry. Add salmon; stir gently to incorporate then form into patties.

Add cooking oil to a large skillet, and heat over medium heat until oil is hot. Add salmon patties and fry until deep golden brown on both sides. Do not overcrowd pan; if necessary, cook in batches. Serve hot.

Prep Time: 15 minutes   Start to Finish: 35 minutes   Servings: 4

Squid & Linguini

Source: Mary Ann Amico

Lucy's note: Aunt Mary Anne used to make this for Uncle Sam quite frequently. She also made this for their restaurant, The Little Club, in Buffalo. Everyone loved her recipe as much as those of us who eat calamari (or squid) do!

5 pounds fresh or frozen squid, also known as calamari - note, if frozen, defrost first.

5 quarts water (very cold)

2 tablespoons lemon juice

2 tablespoons olive oil

1 medium yellow onion, chopped

5 cloves garlic, minced

1 28 oz. can crushed tomatoes

1 1/2 teaspoons sugar

1 teaspoon Italian seasoning

1 tablespoon dried basil

Rinse squid under cold running water for several minutes. Clean out any membrane that may be inside cylinder of body meat. Cut cylinder parts into circles. Tentacles may be left whole or cut into pieces. Place in the 5 quarts of very cold water, to which has been added 2 tbsp. lemon juice.

Heat 1 tbsp. oil in a large pot on medium high. Add chopped onion and minced garlic and sauté until onion is translucent. Add remaining ingredients and 3/4 cup water. Cook at low temperature for one hour.

While sauce cooks, thoroughly rinse squid once more. Sauté in large frying pan to which has been added 1/8 cup water. Simmer for 2 1/2 minutes (do not cook longer as squid will be cooked further in sauce). Remove from heat and set aside.

When sauce is cooked, add squid and simmer for additional 15 minutes. Serve this sauce over linguini.

Serving Ideas: Serve in bowls with lots of fresh Italian bread with which to sop up the sauce. Enjoy!

NOTE: Grandma used to add green peas to her sauce. Add 1 package frozen green peas about 10 minutes before end of cooking time.

Prep Time: 30 minutes   Start to Finish: 1 hour 30 minutes   Servings: 8

Squid Salad

Source: Mary Ann Amico

Lucy's note: This is from Aunt Mary Ann Amico - she and Uncle Sam loved this salad!

2 pounds squid

2 tablespoons lemon juice

2 cups water

1/4 cup white wine

1 Bermuda onion, thinly sliced

2 tablespoons olive oil

1/4 cup lemon juice

salt and pepper

2 tablespoons fresh Italian parsley, chopped

1 tablespoon garlic, minced

4 small tomatoes, chopped

Clean squid by rinsing under cold running water for several minutes. Clean out any membrane that may be inside cylinder of body meat. Place in 5 quarts of very cold water (to which has been added 2 tbsp. lemon juice) for about 15 minutes. Drain thoroughly and cut cylinder part into 1/2 inch rings. Tentacles may be left whole or cut into bite-sized pieces.

In a large pot, bring 2 cups water and white wine to boil along with 1 tablespoon salt. Once boiling, add squid to pot. Bring to a boil again, reduce the heat, and simmer the squid for 1 minute. Drain the squid and cool completely. Add sliced Bermuda onion to squid.

In a small bowl mix together olive oil, 1/4 cup lemon juice, salt, pepper, parsley and garlic. Add to the squid and onion mixture. Toss well, and refrigerate (covered) until ready to serve. Just before serving add tomatoes and bring salad to room temperature.

Prep Time: 25 minutes   Start to Finish: 30 minutes   Servings: 6

Tripe in Marinara Sauce

Source: Phyllis Amico

Vicki's note: This is a recipe that Mom got from Aunt Phyllis many, many years ago. Tripe is not something everyone likes, but those who do truly enjoy!

2 cups marinara sauce, recipe in book

1/2 green bell pepper (diced)

1 celery stalk, chopped small

1 carrot, chopped small

3 pounds tripe, honey comb

4 tablespoons Romano cheese

To prepare tripe, wash tripe thoroughly in cold water. Drain. Remove all visible fat from underside of skin. Wash again. Pat dry. Cut into strips (desired size). Place in 5 quarts of water along with 2 teaspoons salt. Leave in salt water for about 5 minutes. Drain and rinse thoroughly; drain again.

In meantime, bring large pot of water to boil. Place tripe in boiling water. Boil for about 1 1/2 hours on medium heat. While tripe is cooking, prepare marinara sauce according to directions in book, but when cooking onions add bell pepper, celery, and carrot to sauce as noted here.

When tripe is finished boiling, drain thoroughly, rinse in cold water and pat dry. Add to marinara sauce and cook until tender - about 40 minutes. Serve with Romano cheese and lots of crusty Italian bread.

Prep Time: 15 minutes   Start to Finish: 2 hours 30 minutes   Servings: 6

Tuna Casserole

Source: Paul Miller, Sr.

Vicki's note: What would a family cookbook be without this recipe from our child-hood days! This was Dad's specialty when we were kids. Personally, I cannot eat this dish, but apparently I'm in a minority on that one. It is an easy weeknight meal when you have kids to feed.

2 cups egg noodles, cooked

1 8 ounce canned tuna, drained and rinsed

2 tablespoons dried parsley

1/2 cup peas, frozen

1 12 oz. can cream of mushroom soup

1 tablespoon breadcrumbs (or cracker crumbs)

Bring 6 quarts water to boil along with 1 tablespoon salt. Once boiling, cook egg noodles according to package directions.

While pasta is cooking, preheat oven to 400 degrees.

In a small bowl flake tuna with fork (not too finely). Set aside lightly grease an 8" x 8" baking dish. Arrange a layer of 1 cup noodles in dish. Add tuna over noodles; next, sprinkle parsley; then peas, ending with 1 cup noodles. Pour soup over this mixture; sprinkle top with crumbs. Bake in 400 degree oven for 20 to 30 minutes or until top is browned and casserole is heated through.

Serving Ideas: You can also add shredded cheddar cheese to this dish if you'd like, just add before pouring soup over dish.

Prep Time: 20 minutes   Start to Finish: 40 minutes   Servings: 4

Back row: Lee Joe Amico, Paul, Cheryl Amico, Paul Miller Sr. Cynthia Starr,
Paul Miller, Carol Miller, Mike Peters
Front row: Marshall and Lucy Peters, Virginia Amico, Harry Miller, Marianne
Giambroni, Leah Miller, Vicki McNickle, Taylor Suiter, Len Miller, Peg Miller
Thanksgiving – mid 1990's

Soups / Stews

Kelsey, Vicki, Tim, Kari, Taylor and Lucy
Florence Italy, 2006
Wine tasting in the outskirts of Florence in the Chianti Region
It was so wonderful for us to get to spend this time in Italy with Mom!

Bean Soup

Source: Sally Tudini

3 slices bacon

1 tablespoon olive oil

2 cloves garlic, minced

1 medium onion, chopped

1 stalk celery, chopped

2 medium carrots, chopped

28 oz canned crushed tomatoes

2 24 oz cans chicken
broth, low sodium

3 cups water

1 teaspoon dry thyme or sage

1 teaspoon salt

1/2 teaspoon pepper

1 16 oz canned cannellini
beans, rinsed and drained

1 16 oz canned kidney beans,
rinsed and drained

1 16 oz canned garbanzo
beans, rinsed and drained

2 tablespoons Fresh parsley
or combination of parsley
and basil, chopped. If using
dry, add with tomatoes and,
reduce to 1 tablespoon

1 cup frozen green
beans, optional

Chop bacon. Sauté in large pot until crispy, remove from pan and let drain on paper towel. Leave grease from bacon in pan.

Add oil to same pot and heat on medium low for about one minute. Add onion, celery, carrots. Sauté until onions are translucent - 5-10 minutes. Add garlic, and cook 1 minute longer. Add tomatoes, chicken broth and water, and thyme or sage, salt and pepper. If using dried parsley, add now, if using fresh, add in next step. Turn up heat to medium high, and bring to a boil, stirring occasionally. Reduce heat to simmer and continue cooking covered for about 30 minutes. Stir occasionally while cooking.

Add drained and rinsed beans, parsley (if using fresh) and green beans (if using) and continue simmering until beans are heated through - about 10-15 minutes. Remove from heat. Serve with crusty bread.

Serving Ideas: This soup freezes well. Defrost (in refrigerator) before reheating.

Servings: 8

Beef and Bean Chili

Source: Len & Astrid Amico

1 tablespoon oil

1 1/2 pounds ground sirloin
or ground round

1 large onion, finely chopped

2 medium green bell peppers,
finely chopped

1 28 oz. can crushed tomatoes

1 12 oz. can Rotel diced
tomato & green chili, mild,
medium or hot - to taste

1 12 oz. bottle beer

1 16 oz. can: black beans,
rinsed and drained

1 16 oz. can navy beans,
rinsed and drained

1 16 oz. can kidney beans,
rinsed and drained

1 16 oz. can great northern
beans, rinsed and drained

1 16 oz. can pinto beans,
rinsed and drained

1 tablespoon cumin

1 tablespoon Jamaican
jerk spice (or sauce)

1/2 tablespoon paprika

1/2 tablespoon garlic powder

1 teaspoon oregano

1 teaspoon thyme

dash Maggi seasoning, soy sauce
can be substituted

1 1/2 teaspoons salt, to taste

3/4 teaspoon pepper

In a large 8 to 10 quart pot heat oil on medium. Add meat and cook until browned, breaking up as you are cooking. Once browned, add onion and bell pepper and cook additional 5 minutes. Add remaining ingredients, stir well. Cover pot and simmer on medium low heat for 60 minutes.

Serving Ideas: 1 habanero pepper (seeded and chopped) may be added, if you like a lot of heat. Morning Star makes a vegetarian beef that you can use in this to create a vegetarian version. This chili freezes well, so don't be shy about making a large batch.

Servings: 10

Beef Stew

Source: Rosie Giambroni

Vicki's note: This stew reminds me of cold winter nights in Buffalo. This recipe is from Aunt Rosie.

2 tablespoons oil, for browning beef

1 pound beef chuck, cut into 2" cubes

2 16 oz. cans beef broth, low sodium

1 cup water

1 onion, chopped

1 stalk celery, chopped

3 carrots, chopped

2 potatoes, cubed

2 tablespoons fresh parsley, or 1 tbsp dried

1/2 teaspoon garlic powder

1 teaspoon salt

3/4 teaspoon pepper

1/2 cup water

2 tablespoons flour

Heat oil in large pot on medium high heat. Salt and pepper beef, and add to pot - cooking until browned on all sides. NOTE: Do not over crowd pan - you may need to brown beef in batches so beef will actually brown and not steam.

Add onion, broth and 1 cup water. Adjust heat to low and simmer until meat is tender, about 2 hours.

Add remaining ingredients and cook until veggies are tender; about 30 to 40 minutes.

Mix flour and water together to make a watery paste. Add to stew and simmer until stew is thickened. Because the beef broth has salt in it, it's a good idea to taste before adding additional salt.

NOTE: Beef stock may be used (2 cups) instead of broth, or the equivalent made from beef bouillon.

Prep Time: 20 minutes

Servings: 4

Chicken Soup

Source: Lucy Peters

Vicki's note: This recipe is originally from Grandma Amico. Mom tells me it was a traditional Saturday meal when she was growing up. See note below on adding a beef bone to the pot when cooking chicken - this does add a really nice flavor to the soup.

A few notes from Mom (Lucy) on this recipe:
Grandma Amico used to add a beef soup bone to the soup pot with the chicken. After the soup was cooked, Grandma used to take the beef bone out of the pot and Grandpa and I would share the meat and "gado" from the bone (with lots of black pepper). When Uncle Joe was home, it would be a three way grab.

If Grandma could manage to some beef from the bone, she would shred it and about 1/2 of the chicken meat to make a salad. The salad was usually lettuce, onion, garlic, oregano, olive oil and wine vinegar. Sometimes she would add chopped Italian-style green olives to the salad. The salad can be made with the chicken meat only. It's very delicious!

1 whole chicken, cut up

2 15 oz. cans chicken broth

3 stalks celery, chopped

3 medium carrots, chopped

2 medium onions, chopped

3 tablespoons fresh parsley, or 2 tbsp dried

1 1/2 teaspoons salt, more to taste if needed

1 teaspoon pepper

Rinse chicken under cold water, cutting off excess fat. Discard giblets and neck. Place chicken and broth in large pot - cover with cold water to 2 inches above chicken. If using beef bone, add at same time as chicken. Bring to boil, reduce heat, cover and simmer until chicken is half cooked (about 30 minutes). Skim off scum as it rises to top.

Add vegetables; simmer until they are crispy tender and chicken is thoroughly cooked (about 30 minutes). Remove chicken from pot, let cool and debone. Shred chicken and return to pot. Simmer additional 10 minutes.

Serve over rice or ditalini pasta cooked in separate pot. Sprinkle with Romano cheese if desired.

Serving Ideas: When storing soup, don't include pasta as it will absorb all the liquid. I often will use some of the chicken to put into a salad made of romaine lettuce, with Italian dressing and sprinkled with some Romano cheese - very yummy!

Escarole Bean Soup

Source: Sally Tudini

Vicki's note: This recipe is from Aunt Sally. It is originally from Grandma Vaccalluzzo, Grandma Amico's mother.

2 tablespoons olive oil

1 medium onion, finely chopped

2 cloves garlic, minced

2 carrots, peeled and cut into 1/4" slices

1 potato, peeled and diced

2 16 oz. cans chicken broth

2 cups water

1 head escarole, well washed, tough outer leaves removed and coarsely chopped

1/2 teaspoon salt

1/4 teaspoon pepper

1/2 teaspoon thyme

2 16 oz. cans cannellini beans, rinsed and drained

1/4 cup grated Romano or Parmesan cheese, to be served on the side

In a large sauce pan, heat oil on low heat. Sauté onion and garlic in oil for 1 minute. Add carrots and potato along with broth and water. Add escarole, cover and let come to a boil. Lower to simmer and continue cooking for 45 minutes. Add beans and cook for an additional 15 minutes. If you like a thinner soup, add additional broth or water. Sprinkle with grated Parmesan or Romano cheese before serving

Variations:

1. Spinach can be used instead of Escarole - add 1 cup of spinach at the same time as the beans.

2. Add a couple links of Italian sausage at the same time as the onion and garlic. Brown the meat well, then add remainder of ingredients.

3. Cooked meatballs can also be added at the same time as the beans.

Serving Ideas: This soup is yummy served along with crusty Italian bread.

Prep Time: 15 minutes   Start to Finish: 45 minutes   Servings: 4

French Asparagus Bisque

Source: Sally Tudini

2 pounds asparagus, cut into
   1" pieces

2 tablespoons butter

4 medium shallots,
   finely chopped

1 medium potato,
   peeled and diced

3 16 oz. cans chicken
   broth, low sodium

1 teaspoon salt

1/2 teaspoon pepper

1/2 teaspoon
   Worcestershire sauce

1/2 teaspoon dill

2 egg yolks, beaten slightly

1/2 cup whipping cream

2 tablespoons fresh parsley or
   chives, for garnish (optional)

Prepare asparagus by removing tough stems; wash and cut into 1 inch pieces. Set aside. Heat butter over low-medium heat in large pot; add shallots and sauté until translucent. Add asparagus, chicken broth, salt, pepper, Worcestershire sauce, and dill. Simmer until asparagus is very tender, about 30 minutes.

Remove from heat, allow to cool for about 10 minutes, then pour into blender. While soup is cooling, combine egg yolks with cream. Set aside. Blend asparagus mixture until smooth and return mixture to pot; stir in egg yolks and cream mixture. Heat through on low heat, stirring continuously. DO NOT boil or soup will curdle. Garnish with parsley and serve.

Prep Time: 15 minutes   Start to Finish: 40 minutes   Servings: 6

Lentil and Ham Soup

Source: Sam Scarp Elli

Vicki's note: Sam Scarpelli is what I call my "4th brother". He has been a dear friend of Mom's for many years. He was there for her - to go shopping, fix things around the house, drink coffee, smoke cigarettes, share recipes or learn how to professionally decorate cakes! This recipe is from his grandma Gendusa.

2 tablespoons olive oil

1 large yellow onion, chopped

4 carrots, chopped

4 stalks celery, chopped

1 large leek, chopped

2 cloves garlic, minced

4 cups chicken stock or broth

4 cups water

1 1/2 cups brown lentils

1/2 cup green split peas

2 cups ham, chopped,
     or 1 ham bone

2 cups tomatoes, chopped or
     2 cups canned

1/2 teaspoon dried oregano

3 tablespoons fresh Italian
     parsley, or 1 1/2 tbsp. dried

1 bay leaf

2 teaspoons salt

1 teaspoon pepper

1 tablespoon red wine vinegar

8 tablespoons Parmesan
     cheese, grated for topping

Put lentils and split peas in a colander and sort through to check for debris and discard. Then run under cold water and set aside.

Heat oil in a large pot over medium heat. Add chopped onion, celery, leek, carrots and minced garlic and sauté for 6 to 7 minutes. Add stock, water, lentils, split peas, ham hock, oregano, parsley, bay leaf and ham. Bring to a boil, reduce heat to simmer, cover and cook for 1 hour, stirring occasionally.

If using, remove ham bone from soup, cut off ham, discard bone, and return ham to pot. Stir in vinegar, salt and pepper, and simmer an additional 10 minutes longer. Remove bay leaf and discard. Ladle into bowls, drizzle with a little olive oil, and sprinkle with Parmesan cheese.

Serving Ideas: For vegetarian version, use vegetable stock or water instead of chicken stock, and omit the bone.

Servings: 8

Lentil Soup

Source: Lucy Peters

Lucy's note: This is another one of Grandma Amico's famous Friday night meals and/or Wednesday during Lent. She would often make a homemade tagliatelle pasta to serve with the lentils. Her original recipe was made with pork hocks or pig skin. I changed it to bacon and later on eliminated the ham altogether (although I still now and then will use ham - in which case I omit the salt and add to taste at the end. Remove the ham hock before adding spinach).

1 pound lentils

2 strips bacon, optional

1 medium yellow onion, chopped fine

2 medium carrots, chopped

2 stalks celery, chopped

1 clove garlic, minced

3 15 oz. cans low sodium chicken broth

2 cups water

1 teaspoon salt

1/2 teaspoon pepper

2 1/2 cups fresh spinach, package of frozen that has been thawed can be substituted.

Rinse and drain lentils. Look for stones or other debris and discard. Set aside.

Cut bacon into 3 or 4 inch pieces. Fry in large pot over medium heat stirring frequently until crisp. Remove from pot with slotted spoon; set aside. Discard all but 1 tsp. of bacon drippings. If not using bacon, use 1 tbsp. olive oil.

Add onion, carrots and celery to pot; sauté until onion is translucent. About a minute before done, add garlic.

Add broth, water, lentils, salt and pepper to pot. Bring to boil, reduce heat and simmer for about 45 minutes or until lentils are tender. Add spinach during last 10 minutes of cooking.

Lentils can be served over rice or ditalini pasta. Try this for a real taste treat: Drizzle 1 tsp. olive oil over each serving of soup (at serving time).

Prep Time: 15 minutes   Start to Finish: 1 hour   Servings: 6

Minestrone

Source: Lucy Peters

Lucy's note: Grandma made this very often. In those days, frozen foods were just being introduced, so all veggies were fresh. The beans were something I added to Grandma's original recipe. The only beans she added were fresh green beans (in season) or fresh peas (also in season). Otherwise she "cleaned the refrigerator" and used any vegetable she could find. This has always been one of my favorite "comfort foods."

2 teaspoons olive oil

1 large yellow onion, chopped

2 cloves garlic, minced

3 carrot, chopped

2 stalks celery, chopped

1 28 oz. can diced tomatoes

1 tablespoon dried parsley

1 bay leaf

1/2 teaspoon Italian seasoning

1/2 teaspoon dried mint

1/8 teaspoon thyme

1 teaspoon salt

1/2 teaspoon pepper

4 14 oz. cans chicken broth

2 cups broccoli flowerets, or

1 1/2 cups frozen

1 cup cauliflower flowerets,
   or 3/4 cup frozen

1 10 3/4 oz. can corn

1 15 oz. can kidney beans,
   drained and rinsed

1 15 oz. can garbanzo beans

1 15 oz. can cannellini beans, drained and rinsed

1 1/2 cups spinach leaves, or

 1 cup frozen

1/2 cup frozen lima beans (optional)

5 cups cooked pasta, ditalini or
   elbow macaroni are best

5 tablespoons Romano cheese

Heat olive oil in large pot over med-low heat. Add onions, carrots and celery. Sauté over medium low heat until onions are translucent, about 8 to 10 minutes. Add garlic and sauté 1 minute, add tomatoes, chicken broth, 1 cup water and all seasonings. Bring to low boil, then reduce heat to simmer. Simmer for about 30 minutes, stirring occasionally. Add chopped broccoli and cauliflower and continue to simmer for additional 20 minutes or until broccoli and cauliflower are tender. Add the corn and the beans together and heat through, about 10 minutes. Add spinach and continue cooking another 5 minutes. Ideally, you want to allow minestrone to stand for several hours or overnight (in refrigerator) to allow flavors to blend.

In the last half hour of cooking, put on a large pot of water to boil for cooking pasta. Cook per package instructions, drain and sprinkle with some olive oil to keep from sticking together. Ladle 1/2 cup pasta into bowls and cover with one to one and a half cups soup. Serve with Romano cheese on the side for sprinkling on top.

Serving ideas: If you have left over spaghetti sauce, you can use this in place of the tomatoes. Other greens may also be added to soup i.e., any leafy greens. Also, any leftover vegetable broth can be added. A nice addition is to also add a few teaspoons of pesto sauce to the pot just before serving. Avoid adding pasta to the soup, unless you're going to use all at once, as the pasta will become over cooked and absorb the liquid in the soup. This soup also freezes very well.

Vicki's note: A pot of minestrone is usually made the day before everyone starts showing up for Thanksgiving so there is an easy meal available for you to eat whenever you arrive at Mom's.

Prep Time: 30 minutes   Start to Finish: 1 hour 30 minutes   Servings: 10

Pasta Fagioli Soup
Cannellini Bean Soup with Pasta
Source: Joseph Amico

Vicki's note: This recipe is from Uncle Joe, and it's wonderful. The addition of the sausage came from a restaurant in North Beach in SF - it adds a nice flavor. My husband Tim loves this soup - especially when made with fresh beans (see serving suggestions) and sausage.

2 tablespoons olive oil

1 medium onion, finely chopped

2 carrots, finely chopped

2 stalks celery, finely chopped

2 garlic cloves, minced

1 28 oz. can crushed tomatoes

1 tablespoon dried basil

1 teaspoon dried parsley

1 bay leaf

2 16 oz. cans chicken broth

1 teaspoon salt

1/2 teaspoon pepper

2 links sweet Italian
    sausage (optional)

2 16 oz. cans cannellini beans,
    drained and rinsed

1/2 pound small pasta or pastina

4 teaspoons grated Romano
    cheese, or grated
    Parmesan cheese

Heat olive oil in a large pot; add onion, carrots and celery and sauté until onion is translucent, but not browned (about 5 to 8 minutes). Add garlic and sauté for 1 minute more.

If using Italian sausage, while onion, celery and carrots are cooking do the following: remove sausage meat from casing and sauté in pan with a little oil until cooked through, about 10 minutes. Add sausage to pot with tomatoes in next step.

To the onions and vegetables, add crushed tomatoes and spices through pepper and simmer for 30 minutes. Add chicken broth and simmer for 15 minutes more. Add beans and cook until heated through, about 10 minutes. Remove bay leaf from pot. In small batches puree 1/2 of the soup in a separate bowl using an immersion blender, or other such device. Return to pot.

Once you have added chicken broth to vegetables, put water on to boil for pasta with 1 tablespoon salt. Once boiling cook pasta per package directions. Drain in colander.

Serve 1/2 cup pasta in bowls, top with soup, and 1 teaspoon grated cheese if desired.

Serving Ideas: Another recipe I have for this soup came from my girlfriend Lee Ann Giglio, and she actually makes the beans from scratch using great northern beans. The ingredients are pretty much the same with the addition of ham hocks and the cooking time is longer. This is our favorite way to have this soup!

Soak beans in 8 cups of water overnight. Drain and rinse. In a large pot, heat olive oil on medium high, add onion, celery, and carrots - cook for 8 minutes. Add garlic and cook 1 minute longer. Add crushed tomatoes, 4 cups chicken broth and 4 cups water, 2 ham hocks, beans, basil, parsley, bay leaf, salt and pepper. Bring to boil, then reduce heat and simmer for 2 1/2 hours stirring often. Remove ham hock; puree 1/2 of soup then return to pot. Cut ham off of bone and return to pot. Add pasta as with recipe here.

Prep Time: 20 minutes   Start to Finish: 1 hour 20 minutes   Servings: 4

Roasted Butternut Squash and Apple Soup

Source: Vicki McNickle

Vicki's note: This recipe is a combination of a few different recipes I've come across that has morphed into my own version. Tim and the kids love this soup in the winter time - a real comfort food.

1 4lb. butternut squash, peeled, cut in half and seeds removed

2 granny smith apple

2 medium yellow onions

3 tablespoons olive oil

3 teaspoons salt, divided use

1 teaspoon pepper, divided use

3 cups chicken stock

1/8 teaspoon ground nutmeg

1/2 teaspoon ground curry powder

4 tablespoons sour cream, optional

4 tablespoons roasted salted cashews, optional

Preheat oven to 425 degrees

Cut the butternut squash, onions, and apples into 1-inch cubes. Place them on a sheet pan and toss them with the olive oil, 2 teaspoons salt, and 1/2 teaspoon pepper. Divide the squash mixture between 2 sheet pans (lined with parchment or aluminum foil to save on cleanup) and spread in a single layer. Roast for 35 to 45 minutes, tossing occasionally, until very tender. Switch racks half way through cooking time.

Meanwhile, heat the chicken stock to a simmer. When the vegetables are done, put them through a food mill fitted with the medium blade or a potato ricer in batches. The other option is to place the roasted vegetables in batches in a food processor fitted with the steel blade. Add some of the chicken stock and coarsely puree. When all of the vegetables are processed, place them in a large pot and add enough chicken stock to make a thick soup. Add the nutmeg, curry powder, 1 teaspoon salt, and 1/2 teaspoon pepper. Taste for seasonings to be sure there's enough salt and pepper to bring out the curry flavor. Reheat and serve hot with sour cream and roasted salted cashews on the side if desired.

Prep Time: 15 minutes   Start to Finish: 1 hour 15 minutes   Servings: 6

Split Pea Soup

Source: Lucy Peters

Lucy's note: This is another of Grandma Amico's Friday night or Wednesday night meals during Lent.

1 pound split peas

1 tablespoon olive oil

1 large yellow onion, chopped fine

2 large carrots, chopped medium

2 stalks celery, chopped medium

8 cups chicken broth

1 1/2 pounds ham hock

1 tablespoon dried parsley

1 bay leaf

1/4 teaspoon thyme

1 teaspoon salt

1/2 teaspoon black pepper

Rinse split peas under cold water in colander - look for stones or other debris and discard. Set split peas aside.

Heat 1 tbsp oil in large pot. Add onion, carrot, celery and sauté on medium heat until onions are translucent - about 8 to 10 minutes.

Add chicken broth, ham hock, peas and herbs to pot. Bring to boil over medium high heat. Lower heat to simmer and cook the soup, covered, until peas are tender (about 1 1/2 hours). Remove from heat, remove bay leaf and ham hock. When ham hock is cool enough to be handled, remove bone, fat, skin and meat. Cut meat into cubes and set aside.

Puree the soup in batches in a blender. Return to the pot along with the meat and adjust salt and pepper to taste. Heat through to simmer. Serve hot.

Serving Ideas: I've sometimes served this soup over either rice or very small pasta (such as acini di peppe).

Strataccella Soup

Source: Lucy Peters

Lucy's note: I don't recall if Grandma made this soup exactly as I have it here. She did, however, make one with dandelion greens. She used to add them to leftover chicken soup or beef soup, adding pieces of beef or chicken (depending on the soup). It was very good!

6 cups chicken broth

1/2 cup water

1/2 teaspoon salt

3 eggs, slightly beaten

1/4 cup Romano cheese, grated

2 tablespoons fresh parsley, chopped

2 pounds fresh spinach, cut in strips, or 1 pre-packaged bag chopped

1/4 teaspoon pepper

Bring the broth to a boil in a large saucepan over medium high heat.

In a bowl, whisk the eggs, cheese, and parsley to blend. Once broth is boiling, reduce the heat to medium- low. Stir the broth in a circular motion. Gradually drizzle the egg mixture into the moving broth, stirring gently with a fork to form thin strands of egg, about 1 minute. Stir in the spinach, then season soup with salt and pepper to taste.

Ladle soup into individual bowls. Sprinkle with additional cheese.

Serving Ideas: NOTE: Very thin pasta may be added. Break it up and cook al dente. Add to soup just before serving.

Prep Time: 20 minutes   Start to Finish: 25 minutes   Servings: 6

Sweet Potato and Red Lentil Soup

Source: Lucy Peters

Vicki's note: Mom came up with this recipe several years ago and it is now one of my favorites. It is very easy and fast to make.

2 cups red lentils

2 tablespoons vegetable oil

1 medium yellow onion, finely chopped

2 tablespoons fresh ginger, peeled and minced (divided use)

2 cups sweet potatoes, peeled and cubed in 1/2" cubes

4 cups chicken broth

3 cups water

1 teaspoon salt

1/2 teaspoon pepper

Rinse lentils in colander under cold water, removing any stones or other debris. Set aside.

In a large pot, heat oil on medium heat and sauté the onion in oil until translucent, about 5 to 8 minutes. After onions have been in pot about 1 minute, add 1 1/2 tablespoons of the ginger. Once onions are translucent, add the lentils, sweet potato, broth, water, salt and pepper. Increase heat to medium high, and bring soup to a boil, then reduce to low simmer. Cook for about 20 to 25 minutes until the lentils and sweet potatoes are soft. If the soup gets too thick, add a little more water. During the last five minutes of cooking, add an additional 1/2 tablespoon ginger.

Remove soup from heat, let cool for about 10 minutes, then puree half of the soup with immersion blender or blender. Add back to remaining soup. Heat through again if too cool.

Serving Ideas: Can be served with rice (white or brown) or just by itself. If you serve with rice, it will stretch to serve more people.

Zuppa Di Ceci

Garbanzo Bean Soup
Source: Sally Tudini

Vicki's note: This recipe is from Grandma Amico.

1 tablespoon olive oil

3 anchovy fillets, from 2 oz. can,
   packed in oil, bones removed

1 clove garlic, minced

1 16 oz. can crushed tomatoes

1 can chicken broth, low sodium

1/4 teaspoon salt

1/4 teaspoon Italian seasoning

1/8 teaspoon pepper

1 cup pasta, ditalini
   or small elbow

1 16 oz. can garbanzo beans,
   rinsed and drained

4 tablespoons Parmesan
   cheese, grated

Bring 3 quarts of water to which 1 teaspoon of salt has been added, to a boil for cooking pasta.

In the meantime, heat oil in 4 quart pot over low heat. Add anchovies (if they didn't come deboned, remove any small bones before adding to pan), let heat up 2 minutes, then mash with a wooden spoon - they will essentially "melt" in the pan. Once the anchovies are melted (some small pieces will remain), add the garlic and sauté 1 minute more. Add tomatoes, chicken broth, salt, pepper and Italian seasoning. Increase heat to medium high and bring to a low boil. Reduce heat to low and simmer mixture for 30 minutes, stirring occasionally.

10 minutes before end of cooking time, start pasta per package instructions.

5 minutes before the tomatoes and chicken broth are finished cooking, add the garbanzo beans. If you have chosen to add greens (see serving ideas) then this is the time to add those as well. Continue to simmer until beans are heated through and greens are wilted, if using.

Pour 1 1/2 cups of soup over 1/2 cup pasta in bottom of bowl. Serve with Parmesan on the side.

Serving Ideas: Various leafy vegetables may be added to the soup, such as chopped spinach, Swiss chard, escarole, etc. About 1 1/2 cups of chopped vegetables should be enough. If not finishing at once, store pasta and soup separate as the pasta will absorb all the liquid in the soup.

Prep Time: 15 minutes   Start to Finish: 45 minutes   Servings: 4

Vegetables

Lucy & her best friend Virginia Amico, who is also my Aunt Gina
She contributed many recipes in this book!
Summer, 2009

Artichokes Stuffed (Sicilian Style)

Source: Lucy Peters

Lucy's note: Grandma Amico made artichokes quite frequently when they were in season. I like making these because they bring back "Grandma's Kitchen" memories.

4 artichokes, see note about choosing artichokes

1 tablespoon lemon juice

2 cups breadcrumbs, Italian flavored

4 cloves garlic, minced

1/4 cup Romano cheese

1 teaspoon dried mint

1 teaspoon dried parsley

4 tablespoons olive oil

Combine 1 quart water and lemon juice in a large pot. Set aside.

Remove tough outer leaves from bottom of artichokes. Cut off stem and top 1 inch of artichoke. With scissors, cut sharp tips off remaining leaves. Rub tops of each artichoke with cut lemon to prevent discoloration. Gently spread artichoke leaves to allow room for stuffing. Rinse in cold water. Shake out excess water. Place artichokes in the water with lemon juice bath.

In a small bowl (large enough to get your hand in), combine breadcrumbs, garlic, Romano cheese, mint and parsley.

Remove artichokes from bath and drain upside down for a couple of minutes on paper towel. Fill the center and each leaf with a bit of the bread crumb mixture, starting in the middle and working your way out. Gently pull the leaves apart as you fill them in order to get filling down close to the bottom of each leaf. Place artichokes in empty pot large enough to accommodate all four artichokes once stuffed (figure about 4 inches each.) They should fit snuggly. Add enough room temperature water to cover bottom 1/4 of artichokes. Drizzle 1 tbsp. olive oil over each. Place pot over medium heat, cover and bring water to boil. Lower heat and simmer artichokes for 45 minutes to one hour. Cooking time will depend on the size of the artichokes.

Artichokes are cooked when a center leaf can be easily pulled out (use tongs) and heart is easily pierced with a fork. Test for doneness after about 45 minutes.

Serving Ideas: When artichokes are fresh, the leaves are compact and close. If leaves are spread, it is an indication of artichokes that have passed their prime.

Prep Time: 15 minutes   Servings: 4

Black Eyed Peas

Source: Denny McGinnis

Vicki's note: My dear friend Denny makes these black eyed peas every New Years Eve, and generously shares them with us as "good luck" for the new year. They are wonderful!

1 pound black eyed peas

2 tablespoons baking soda

1 ham hock

1 package center-cut ham bone

1 large yellow onion,
   chopped fine

1 teaspoon salt

1/4 teaspoon pepper

1/8 teaspoon cayenne

Pour peas into a colander and sort through to remove any debris or stones. Then rinse peas under cold water. Place peas in large pot covered with cold water by 2 inches. Stir in baking soda. Soak peas over night or for 8 hours. Pour out water, rinse peas well.

Place black eyed peas, ham and onion in large pot with enough water to cover. Bring to a boil, reduce heat to simmer and cook uncovered 1 1/2 hours. Add salt, pepper and cayenne; stir and serve.

Servings: 8

Breaded Baked Eggplant

Source: Sally Tudini

1 pound eggplant, cut into 1/4 " slices
1 teaspoon salt
1/4 teaspoon pepper
1 egg (or 2 egg whites)
1 cup Italian breadcrumbs
3 tablespoons butter

Preheat oven to 400 degrees. Line baking sheet with aluminum foil which has been lightly coated with cooking spray.

Peel eggplant and cut into 1/4 inch slices. Sprinkle with salt and place in colander for about 1/2 hour to drain. This process removes the bitterness from the eggplant. Rinse eggplant slices with cool water and pat dry.

Beat eggs with pepper in a shallow bowl large enough for dipping eggplant. Put breadcrumbs in shallow bowl large enough for dipping eggplant. Dip eggplant into beaten egg and then bread crumbs. Place on large dish and allow to "rest" for about 15 minutes, then place on lightly greased baking sheet.

Dot tops of each slice of eggplant with butter and bake in 400 degree oven for 40 minutes or until browned.

Serving Ideas: This can be served as a nice side dish with any meal.

Candied Yams

Source: Sandy Amico

Vicki's note: This recipe is part of my childhood memories and holidays spent with my Uncle Angelo and his family. Aunt Sandy used to make these at Thanksgiving and I loved them. What kid doesn't love vegetables with marshmallows in them! Though the marshmallows are optional, if you have children, they're a must. Our family has eliminated the maple syrup from this recipe and uses more brown sugar.

8 yams, or sweet potatoes
   salt and pepper, sprinkled
   between layers

1/2 cup brown sugar, If
   not using maple syrup,
   increase this to 3/4 cup

6 tablespoons butter

1/4 cup maple syrup,
   optional (see above note
   on brown sugar)

1 cup miniature marshmallows

Preheat oven to 325 degrees. Butter bottom and sides of a 9" x 13" baking dish (butter spray may be used). Set baking dish aside.

Wash yams and place in large pot of cold water (with skins on). If yams are large, cut in half before boiling-you want them to be around the same size to ensure even cooking. Bring water to a boil and cook until almost done - 30 to 45 minutes - you should be able to insert a knife into them easily, but they should still be a bit firm and not mushy. Cool, peel and slice into 1/2 inch slices.

Place a layer of yams in bottom of prepared baking dish. Sprinkle with salt and pepper; then sprinkle with 1/4 cup of the brown sugar; next place small pieces of the butter - about 3 tablespoons broken into small pieces - over top. Continue layering, ending with butter pieces. Pour maple syrup over all. If using more brown sugar instead of maple syrup, then you will top with remaining brown sugar. Place dish in oven.

Bake for 1/2 hour. Remove from oven and top with marshmallows. Return to oven until marshmallows are browned - 5 to 10 minutes. Serve hot.

Prep Time: 45 minutes

Servings: 12

Chestnut Stuffing

Source: Lucy Peters

Vicki's note: Thanksgiving is the ultimate holiday in our family. This stuffing is one of Mom's hallmark dishes! When Paul and I were little we were the chestnut peelers. If you have ever peeled chestnuts you know this is no easy job! We find joy in sharing this childhood task. We have even been known on occasion to share the joys of this task with our kids. Chestnut stuffing is a traditional Italian recipe.

1 pound chestnuts, or 15 oz. jarred can also be used to cut down prep time.

2 cups celery, diced (roughly 2 to 3 stalks)

2 cups yellow onion, diced (1 large onion or 2 medium)

3/4 cup butter

2 12 oz. packages of herb stuffing mix

1/3 cup fresh parsley, chopped, or 5 tbsp. dried

1 teaspoon salt

1 teaspoon pepper

2 teaspoons poultry seasoning, more if needed

5 cups chicken broth or stock

Preheat oven to 425 degrees.

"Score" bottom of chestnuts by putting a small slit into the lighter color of nut at bottom. Note: If you don't score, they will "pop" from the pressure in the oven. While this can be exciting, it can also be a bit nerve racking! Place in one layer on baking sheet, sprinkle with about 1/4 cup water - you just want to give the pan and nuts a little moisture, you are not covering them in water. Use your hand to sprinkle the water over the nuts. Roast in oven 20 to 25 minutes.

Remove the nuts from the oven, mound them in an old towel, wrap them up, squeeze them hard -- they should crackle. Let them sit for a few minutes; once cool enough to handle, remove skin from nuts. You may be able to do this with your hands, or may want to use a small paring knife to help peel off the skins. Chop nuts into 1/2 inch chunks - doesn't have to be exact, just don't chop them too much. You want nice chunks that you will able to taste in the stuffing. If you don't want to go through this hassle, buy jarred chestnuts.

While the chestnuts are roasting, dice up 2 cups celery and 2 cups yellow onion. In a large pot (big enough to accommodate the two bags of stuffing) melt the 3/4 cup butter, then add the onion and celery and sauté until onions are translucent - about 8 to 10 minutes. Remove from heat. Add stuffing, chopped chestnuts and seasoning to pot - mix well. Add the stock slowly, mixing well as you add each cup. The stuffing should be moist. If more stock is needed, add a little at a time. If you are not going to stuff a bird with the stuffing, then you may want to add more poultry seasoning - this is a personal preference - you'll want to taste it to see if you want more.

Serving Ideas: This recipe will stuff a 20 pound turkey with extra to heat up. You can cut it in half if you want to stuff a chicken or a smaller bird. Homemade turkey stock gives this stuffing a richer flavor, if you choose to use canned chicken broth, especially if it is low sodium, you will want to add more salt, pepper and/or poultry seasoning.

Prep Time: 40 minutes   Start to Finish: 1 hour 40 minutes   Servings: 20

Cuccia

Sicilian Wheat Berries
Source: Lucy Peters

Lucy's note: Grandma Amico used to make this on Santa Lucia's Day - Dec.13. It was quite traditional in most Italian households to serve this wonderful wheat dish on that day. In our household it was unheard of not to have Cuccia on the feast of Santa Lucia. It was quite important for Grandpa and Grandma because I think in their way they were honoring not only the patron saint of sight, but also their first Lucy who was named after this patron saint and who died 5 months before I was born. Although the recipe seems complicated, it is actually quite easy to make and worth the time involved. There are many wonderful memories attached to this dish. Grandma served this to us at breakfast on Santa Lucia's Day with milk and sugar and also after school (as a "snack") drizzled with olive oil and lots of black pepper.

**1 pound wheat berries
  (whole wheat kernels)**

7 cups water

2 teaspoons salt, divided use

1/2 teaspoon pepper

**2 16 oz. cans garbanzo beans,
  drained and rinsed**

It's important to use soft wheat. This can be purchased at any health food store that carries bulk foods.

Rinse the wheat under cold water in a colander. Place in a large pot and add COLD water to about two inches above the berries, add 1 teaspoon salt. Soak overnight or for one full day. Change the water a couple of times during soaking.

Rinse the wheat once more and place in a large heavy pot with the 7 cups of water and 1 teaspoon salt. Cover the pot and bring wheat to boil. Lower heat to simmer and cook for about 1 1/2 hours or until the kernel skins split SLIGHTLY. Stir occasionally during this time. Drain most of the water, leaving just enough to keep the wheat moist.

Wrap the pot, (well sealed with the lid) in a kitchen towel and then in a blanket or old quilt. You'll need at least 2 layers around the pot to keep the heat in, and to let the wheat further tenderize and steam open. It is often good to do this overnight, but at a minimum keep wrapped for five hours.

In the morning or after 5 hours, unwrap the pot and scrape off the top layer of wheat, which will look dry. Underneath you'll find the kernels have popped open. Some of the white interior will show through the brown skin.

Add the garbanzo beans, 1 tsp. salt, and ½ tsp. pepper. Mix gently and store in airtight container in refrigerator.

When ready to serve, take out as much as you think you'll use, heat through, drizzle with olive oil and serve. If you would like to serve this for breakfast, take out as much as you think you'll use, heat through, pour a little milk and sugar over the top and serve.

Serving Ideas: It's best to cook the wheat in the evening because it needs to be "wrapped" overnight.

Prep Time: 15 minutes   Start to Finish: 9 hours 45 minutes   Servings: 10

Eggplant Parmesan (Grandma Amico Style)

Source: Lucy Peters

Lucy's note: This recipe is from Grandma Amico.

1 pound eggplant, cut into
   1/2" slices

2 eggs, beaten

1/4 cup milk

1/2 teaspoon salt

1/4 teaspoon pepper

1 1/2 cups Italian bread crumbs

1 teaspoon dried parsley flakes

1 teaspoon dried mint flakes

1 cup grated Romano
   cheese, divided use

3 tablespoons olive oil

3 cups marinara or meat sauce

Preheat oven to 325 degrees.

Wash eggplant, peel and cut into 1/2 inch slices. Lightly salt both sides of eggplant and place on in a large colander in the sink - try not to "stack" the eggplant. This process pulls out the bitterness of the eggplant. Allow to stand for 1/2 hour, then rinse under cold water and pat dry completely.

In a pie plate or similar dish, mix together eggs, milk, salt and pepper. Put breadcrumbs on a large platter or plate. Add 1/2 cup of the cheese, parsley and mint flakes to the breadcrumbs - stir to combine.

Dip prepared eggplant slices in egg mixture and then in breadcrumb mixture, pressing slightly to make breadcrumbs adhere. Place on platter until all slices are coated.

Heat oil 1 tablespoon at a time in large skillet over medium high heat and cook in batches until lightly browned on both sides. Remove from pan and transfer to paper towel-lined cookie sheet. Add additional oil as needed (make sure additional oil is heated sufficiently before adding more eggplant). When all eggplant has been browned, proceed as directed below.

Spread 3/4 cup of sauce on bottom of an 8" x 8" casserole dish. Next, place 1/3 of the eggplant slices over sauce. Cover with additional sauce. Sprinkle with cheese. Repeat layers ending with sauce and cheese. Cover casserole with aluminum foil and bake for -20 minutes. Remove foil and bake for an additional 10 to 15 minutes until eggplant is tender and sauce is bubbly. Remove from oven, cover with aluminum foil and let stand for about 15 minutes before cutting into squares. Serve with additional sauce and cheese if desired.

Serving Ideas: This makes a wonderful side dish for pasta, meat, chicken or fish. Very tasty the next day as a cold sandwich. (Of course, between 2 slices of crusty bread.)

Prep Time: 45 minutes   Start to Finish: 1 hour 35 minutes   Servings: 6

Florentine Rice Ring

Source: Sally Tudini

Vicki's note: This recipe is from Aunt Sally; originally from her Grandma Rosaria Vaccalluzzo (who was Grandma Amico's mother). It is a GREAT side dish. Makes a lot - so it's especially good when feeding a lot of people. I've also eaten this as a whole meal just by itself.

2 packages frozen chopped spinach

4 cups white rice

8 cups water

1 teaspoon salt

1/2 teaspoon pepper

1/4 teaspoon garlic powder

4 tablespoons butter, separate use

1 1/2 cups Parmesan cheese, grated or shredded

Cook spinach as directed on package. Once cooked, place in colander to remove most of the moisture. Once cool enough to touch, press with hand to remove excess moisture. This is important because you want the spinach to be as "dry" as possible. While spinach is draining prepare remaining ingredients.

In a large pot, stir rice, water, salt, garlic powder and 2 teaspoons butter into sauce pan. Bring to boil, stir, cover and reduce heat to low simmer, place cover on pot and cook for 20 minutes. DO NOT STIR or remove lid during this 20 minutes.

Set aside 2 tablespoons Parmesan cheese (to be used to garnish.) In a large bowl or pot, combine rice, spinach (NOTE: Make sure spinach is fully drained before adding as noted above), remaining 2 tablespoons butter and 1 1/4 cup of cheese. Spoon into 6 cup ring mold sprayed with cooking spray, pressing firmly to set. Hint: Using a 1/2 cup measuring cup with a flat bottom is an easy way to set rice into the ring mold. Cover with aluminum foil. Let stand for 20 minutes.

Unmold ring onto heated serving plate. Sprinkle with reserved 1/4 cup cheese.

Serving Ideas: This makes a great side dish with meatloaf or pork. You can also add 1 pound cooked and crumbled Italian sausage to rice and spinach to create a whole meal in one dish!

Prep time: 30 minutes   Start to Finish: 1 hour 20 minutes   Servings: 16

Garlic Mashed Potatoes

Source: Vicki McNickle

Vicki's note: This is one of those good recipes I picked up along the way.

6 large russet potatoes

6 medium garlic cloves

1 tablespoon salt

3 tablespoons butter

1/3 cup milk, or heavy cream;
slightly warmed (not boiling)

3 tablespoons sour cream

1 teaspoon salt, or to taste

1/2 teaspoon pepper, or to taste

parsley, optional for garnish

Peel potatoes, chop into 1 inch cubes. Place in large pot of cold water (enough to cover potatoes plus 2 inches) along with garlic and 1 tablespoon salt. Bring to boil on high heat. Reduce heat to medium and continue cooking until potatoes are soft when fork is inserted into middle (20 to 30 minutes).

Drain potatoes in colander and return to pot. Add butter. Mash a bit until butter is melted. Add milk gradually along with sour cream, salt and pepper. Continue to mash until lumps are gone. Serve hot with a little parsley sprinkled on top for garnish.

Prep Time: 10 minutes   Start to Finish: 45 minutes   Servings: 6

Grilled Asparagus and Melon Salad

Source: Vicki McNickle

Vicki's note: This is a tasty vegetable dish I modified from a recipe I found some-where. Very tasty and refreshing!

2 ounces prosciutto

2 tablespoons pine nuts, toasted

1 pound asparagus, trimmed

3 tablespoons extra virgin
   olive oil, separate use

1/2 teaspoon salt

1/4 teaspoon pepper

2 tablespoons fresh lemon juice

1/4 cantaloupe melon, peeled,
   seeded and cut into 3/4" cubes

4 ounces fresh mozzarella,
   cut into 3/4" cubes

Place oven rack in center of oven. Preheat the oven to 350 degrees.

Line a baking sheet with parchment. Place the pro-sciutto in a single layer on the baking sheet. Bake in preheated oven for 12 to 14 minutes until crispy. Chop into 1/4 inch pieces.

Meanwhile, place a grill pan over medium high heat or preheat a gas or charcoal grill. Toss together the asparagus and 1 tablespoon olive oil. Season with salt and pepper. Grill for 2 to 3 minutes each side until slightly tender but still crisp.

While prosciutto cools, place pine nuts onto a cookie sheet, and bake in 350 degree oven for 8 minutes. Let cool completely.

In a medium bowl, whisk together lemon juice and 2 tablespoons olive oil, 1/2 teaspoon salt and 1/4 teaspoon pepper. Toss with the melon and mozzarella cheese until all ingredients are combined.

Arrange the asparagus on a platter and top with the melon and cheese mixture. Drizzle any remaining vinaigrette over the top. Sprinkle with prosciutto and pine nuts and serve.

Prep Time: 15 minutes   Start to Finish: 45 minutes   Servings: 4

Kale or Other "Assertive" Greens

Source: Lucy Peters

Lucy's note: This recipe can also be used for other "hearty" green such as collards, or turnip greens. These greens are referred to as "assertive" greens. They are tougher and require longer cooking time.

2 pounds kale (or other greens listed)

1/2 medium onion (optional), finely chopped

2 medium cloves garlic, minced or pressed

2 tablespoons olive oil

2 quarts water

1 1/2 teaspoons salt

1/4 teaspoon pepper

2 teaspoons cider vinegar (optional)

2 slices bacon (optional), cut into 1" pieces

Wash greens in several changes of cold water. Drain, remove tough spine and stems - discard. Coarsely chop leaves. Heat olive oil in a deep pot over medium heat. Add onion (if using.) sauté until onion is soft. Add garlic and briefly sauté (30 seconds). Add water and salt. Bring to boil. Add kale (or other greens listed above) Bring to a boil. Reduce heat to low; cover pot. Continue cooking, stirring occasionally, until tender - about 20 minutes or more. Add vinegar and cooked bacon if using just before serving. Makes about 2 cups.

NOTE: If using bacon, fry the bacon pieces in a sauté pan over medium heat until crisp (5 minutes). Remove from pan with a slotted spoon; drain on paper towels. Add to greens just before serving.

Prep Time: 30 minutes

Spinach or Other Tender Greens

Source: Lucy Peters

Vicki's note: This recipe can be used for making any "tender greens" such as Swiss chard or mustard greens.

2 pounds spinach, or other greens as listed

3 tablespoons olive oil

2 medium cloves garlic, minced or pressed

1/2 teaspoon salt

1/4 teaspoon pepper

lemon wedges (optional)

Remove stems from spinach. If using Swiss chard, remove tough spine as well before chopping leaves. Wash under cold running water. Shake to remove excess water and coarsely chop. If using bagged spinach, simply add some cold water to bag, shake spinach in bag, and then remove excess water.

Heat oil in deep pot over medium heat. Add garlic; sauté for about 30 seconds. Add wet greens, cover pot. Cook, stirring occasionally, until greens are completely wilted; about 2 or 3 minutes. Remove cover, season with salt and pepper (to taste). If any liquid is remaining in pot, raise heat to high; cook until liquid evaporates (2 or 3 minutes). Serve with lemon wedges (if using). A small amount of olive oil may be drizzled over top, when serving.

Serving Ideas: Also see recipe in this book for "Swiss chard with tomatoes" for another way to enjoy this wonderful green. I will often add 1 teaspoon of white wine or apple cider vinegar to my greens - it gives them a nice added flavor. This would be in place of the lemon.

Prep Time: 10 minutes   Start to Finish: 15 minutes   Servings: 4

Stuffed Eggplant

Source: Sally Tudini

Vicki's note: This recipe is from Aunt Sally Tudini's kitchen. She got this from Julia (my grandma's sister) who brought it here from Sicily when she moved here after my grandmother passed away.

4 Japanese eggplants, or
   small domestic eggplants

1 teaspoon salt

1/2 cup Romano cheese

3 cloves garlic, minced

1/2 cup Italian flavored
   breadcrumbs

1/2 teaspoon pepper

2 teaspoons fresh mint,
   or 1 teaspoon dried

1 4 oz. can anchovies, optional

3 tablespoons olive oil

Preheat oven to 325 degrees. Clean and dry eggplant. Make 3 evenly spaced slits in eggplant (2 if using small eggplants). Sprinkle pocket lightly with salt; set aside.

In a medium bowl, mix cheese, garlic, breadcrumbs, pepper and mint. Fill each pocket with breadcrumb mixture, being careful not to split eggplant. Spray the bottom of a 9"x13" glass baking dish. Place eggplant in baking dish and top each with an anchovy if using. Drizzle olive oil over tops of eggplants.

Pour 1/2 cup water in bottom of baking dish to keep eggplant from drying out. Watch carefully while baking, adding additional water if needed. Bake for 35 to 45 minutes or until tender (when a fork can be inserted easily). Check at 20 minute intervals. If eggplant begins to brown too much, cover lightly with aluminum foil.

When cooked, remove from oven, cover lightly with aluminum foil and allow to rest for about 10 minutes before serving.

Prep Time: 15 minutes   Start to Finish: 1 hour   Servings: 8

Swiss Chard with Tomatoes

Source: Lucy Peters

Lucy's note: Another of Grandma Amico's wonderful vegetable dishes. We all loved Swiss chard served this way.

1 pound Swiss chard

1 tablespoon olive oil

1 small onion, finely chopped

1 clove garlic, finely minced

1 16 oz. can crushed tomatoes

1 teaspoon salt, divided use

1/4 teaspoon pepper

3 tablespoons fresh basil leaves, cut in fine strips, or 1 1/2 tablespoons dried basil

Wash Swiss chard thoroughly under cold running water. Remove stems from leaves; cut into 2 inch pieces. Set aside. Rough chop leaves. Set aside.

In a small pot, bring 1 cup of water to boil over medium heat. Add 1/2 teaspoon salt. Stir in stems; cook for 7 to 8 minutes. Remove stems from cooking water; set aside

In the meantime, place a medium pot over medium low heat. When warmed, add olive oil. Stir in onion, sautéing until onion is translucent - 5 to 8 minutes. Add garlic, continue sautéing for 1 more minute. Add tomatoes, 1/2 teaspoon salt and 1/4 teaspoon pepper and basil leaves. Cook for about 30 minutes. Add chopped Swiss chard leaves and cooked stems. Continue cooking for about 10 minutes longer, or until leaves and stems are tender. Adjust seasonings, if needed. Remove from heat; transfer to a serving bowl.

Serving Ideas: If serving with crusty bread, try "dunking" the bread into the sauce. A real taste treat.

Prep Time: 10 minutes   Start to Finish: 45 minutes   Servings: 4

Zucchini with Tomatoes

Source: Lucy Peters

Vicki's note: This is a Mom "creation". It's delicious!

2 teaspoons olive oil

1 medium onion, finely chopped

2 cloves garlic, minced or pressed

1/2 cup water

4 medium zucchini, cut into
    1/2" round slices

1/2 28 oz. can crushed tomatoes

1/2 packet Italian salad
    dressing, dry mix

Romano cheese, or Parmesan
    for sprinkling on top

Heat olive oil in medium saucepan over medium low heat. Add onion and sauté until translucent, 8 to 10 minutes. Add garlic, sauté for 1 minute. Lower heat to low. Add water and sliced zucchini; cook for 20 minutes, stirring often. Add crushed tomatoes and the 1/2 packet of Italian salad dressing mix - stir well. Reduce heat to simmer. Continue cooking for additional 30 minutes. Taste for seasoning. Additional seasoning will probably not be necessary because of the addition of the salad dressing mix. Serve grated cheese on side for people to add as they like.

Serving Ideas: Serve as a side dish, sprinkled with Romano or Parmesan cheese. This can also be served over pasta for a full meal

Prep Time: 10 minutes   Start to Finish: 40 minutes   Servings: 6

Our Tradition of Thanksgiving

From the time I was very young, Thanksgiving has always been a special holiday for me. The word itself evokes warm emotion. It conjures memories of family, laughter and celebration. A time of sharing and coming together with those I love.

Early on, it was a gathering of all the aunts and uncles and cousins at my Grandparents house; later, it moved to Uncle Angelo and Aunt Sandy's house or our house. The women would cook, and the men would watch football. The children, depending on age, either were relegated to play outside or to help in the kitchen (particularly if you were a girl!) This was ripe territory for learning the cooking techniques of the various women in our family.

While there was much cooking going on in the kitchen, everyone brought something too. Aunt Rosie would bring pie, Aunt Sandy some type of appetizer, Aunt Gina a salad, and so on. In those early days, Grandpa had a wine cellar where he made his own wine, and that was a special part of the meal too. . Aunt Gina recalls that it didn't taste all that great. As a child, I didn't know the difference – I was just thrilled if they let me have a sip! As we gathered, no matter at whose house, there were a lot of people. We would sit in the kitchen, dining room, and living room, and before we ate, we prayed and gave thanks.

As the years progressed and Grandparents passed, as children grew and families moved away, the tradition of this wonderful holiday still remained strong in my family. After Mom and I moved to California in 1977, this holiday became even more important to Mom as her own children were now spread across the western US. She became passionately committed to bringing our family together to continue this wonderful Thanksgiving tradition. She asked that we all make the effort to come together as a family – no matter where we lived, no matter how many children we had– she asked that we please be willing to make the effort to show up for at least this one time of year to be together. We all agreed, and, for the most part, we have kept our promise. This has now become the one time of year when we are all together in one place. I love that we share this tradition and have created it for our children as well – they, too, love this time when we are all together.

Mom loves having all her children home for Thanksgiving. She begins preparations at least a month in advance-- shopping, making sauce, meatballs and manicotti shells and freezing them. The weekend before, I go down to her house and help with shopping, making the cannoli shells and whatever else there is to be done. . On Tuesday, everyone starts arriving, excitement mounts, and fun and laughter begin. Over the years, many of our extended family have joined in the celebrations of the week – Aunt Gina, cousin Cheryl, cousin Mike, cousin Maryanne to name a few.

Tuesday through Friday are filled with food and fun. Any given year may include games, walks on the beach, swimming in the pool, scavenger hunts, card playing, karaoke, dancing, charades, birthday and anniversary celebrations, long walks, long talks, and huge amounts of laughter and love!

One very special tradition Mom began many years ago is a particularly wonderful part of this holiday for us all. After dinner, one by one, we go around the table and share what we are grateful for in the past year. We publicly speak about our gratitude for others around the table – the ways they have touched our lives and brought us joy; for the ways they have taught us and brought us wisdom; for the gifts they have brought that have enriched us. The tears usually begin flowing fairly early on – tears of joy, tears for loss, tears of deep, deep gratitude for the blessings in our lives. It is not always serious though - sometimes people say funny things too, which in the midst of the tears, can be a welcome break.

Starting on Saturday as we wrap up the festivities and begin to disburse, there are promises to call when we arrive at our final destinations and long hugs goodbye. By the end of Sunday, Mom's house is quiet again, and she begins putting it back together again. In some ways sad that we have all left and in other ways glad to have her house back in order!

At this writing, we have had only one Thanksgiving without Mom, and while I'm certain my brothers and I will carry on this very special tradition, it is taking new shape. Last year, we were at Paul's house in Phoenix. While we tried to keep the "routine" the same, the lack of Mom's presence was felt – how she loved this holiday!

This year, we will be celebrating at my home in Northern California – I am thrilled that everyone will be here for this special holiday.

While Mom is not here with us physically, I know she is here in spirit and that she is delighted we are carrying on with the special tradition. Thanksgiving together is a tradition that brings meaning to *all* our lives. It is a unique and special time we share with the people who love us no matter what. Who are there for us in the best of times and the hardest of times – they are our family. *La Familia* – when you're Italian there is no stronger bond than your family. . I'm so grateful to have passed on the legacy of this bond to our children, and I know it will continue to enrich their lives for many years to come.

Vicki

Thanksgiving – Recipe Index

The following recipes are those traditionally made at Thanksgiving in our house. This list is being provided so that when my children and grandchildren are looking to re-create the "experience" these recipes will be here!

Wednesday Night Dinner:
Spaghetti Sauce
Meatballs
Manicotti

Appetizers:
Caponata
Cardoon
Clams Casino

Dinner:
Candied Yams
Turkey with Chestnut Stuffing
Gravy

Desert:
Cannoli
Pumpkin Cheesecake
Pumpkin Ice Cream Pie

Other:
Egg Breakfast Casserole
Potatoes, Sausage and Peppers

Thanksgiving Photos

Vicki, Tim, April, Paul, and Leah
Taking shots of Tequila – a tradition of our Thanksgiving get together!

Len, Pam, Vicki, Tim, Paul, Lucy, April, Harry, Cynthia, and Mike
This is a Thanksgiving in Lake Arrowhead, a place we spent several holidays
over the years.

Thanksgiving –1998

Top Row: Lee Joe Amico, Paul Levy, Cheryl Amico, Paul Miller Sr., Harry &
Cynthia Miller, Paul & Carol Miller, Mike Peters
Bottom Row: Marshall & Lucy Peters, Virginia Amico, Mary Ann Giambroni,
Leah Miller, Vicki Suiter-McNickle, Taylor Suiter, Len & Peg Miller

Thanksgiving 2000

Vicki & Tim McNickle, Taylor Suiter, Harry Miller, Leah Miller, Cynthia Starr,
Kelsey McNickle, Kari McNickle, Len Miller, Peg Miller, Mike Peters
Carlsbad Beach, CA

Thanksgiving 2008

Tradition being passed to the next generation! Sarah and Jessica peeling potatoes!

The family that eats together stays together!
Leah, Carol, Don, April, and Paul

Thanksgiving 2009

Kari, family friend, Jeff, and Kelsey

Vicki, Tim, and Taylor

Thanksgiving 2007

Top – Tim, Leah, Mike, April

2nd Row – Len, Pam, Vicki, Harry, Cynthia, Paul, Liz, Jason

Bottom Row – Sarah, Jon, Carson, Tyler, Lucy, Virginia

Lake Arrowhead, CA – a place where many fond Thanksgiving memories were made!

Visit our blog at: www.mangia-iloveyou.com

You can also email Vicki at: vicki@suiterfinancial.com

Index

Made in the USA
Lexington, KY
20 June 2015